GROW
ALL YOU CAN EAT IN
3 SQUARE FEET

GROW
ALL YOU CAN EAT IN
3 SQUARE FEET

Horticultural Consultant Naomi Schillinger
Senior Editor Chauney Dunford
Senior Art Editor Clare Marshall
Editor Tia Sarkar
Illustrator Bryony Fripp
Senior Jacket Creative Nicola Powling
Jacket Designer Ria Holland
Senior Producer Che Creasey
Pre-production Producer Andy Hilliard
Managing Editor Penny Warren
Publisher Mary Ling
Art Director Jane Bull

First published in Great Britain in 2015 by
Dorling Kindersley Limited
80 Strand, London, WC2R 0RL

16

034–195596–Feb/2015

A CIP catalogue record of this book is available
from the British Library.

ISBN 978-0-2411-8001-3

Printed and bound in China

A WORLD OF IDEAS:
SEE ALL THERE IS TO KNOW
www.dk.com

Contents

MAKING
A START

3 golden rules for growing your own crops

1

GET TO KNOW YOUR PLOT
● Identify every space in your garden where you could grow crops, including in pots, and ensure these areas are suitable for plants (*see pp.14–19*).

2

DECIDE WHAT YOU WANT TO GROW
● Think about the crops you'd like to grow, work out if you have the space (*see pp.32–34*), and can give them the right conditions (*see pp.224–241*).

3

MAXIMIZING YOUR HARVEST
● Make the most of the space and time you have. Start your plants early, keep them healthy, harvest promptly, and re-sow bare spaces (*see pp.42–57*).

Where can I grow crops?

......practically anywhere.

In the soil

If you have space, the **best place** to grow your crops is directly **in the soil.** Choose the best spot possible (*see pp.14–19*), and **make a bed** as large as you need. Get to **know your soil** and **improve it** if you need to (*see pp.18–19*).

Raised beds

Raised beds are a **great option** even if you can **plant directly** in the soil, and they have many **advantages** (*see pp.20–21*). They are also **ideal for spaces** where there is **no earth**, such as on a **patio**, or where the **soil is poor**.

Containers

Most crops can be **grown in pots** as long as they are **large enough** for what you want to grow. Containers are a **great option** for smaller plots, and they can also help you to make **full use** of every space in even **larger gardens**.

Be creative!

By being creative with the **space** you have and **how you use** it, you'll **be surprised** by the amount of crops **you can grow**. Hang saddle bags over your **balcony**, line your **paths** with pots, and **fix shelves** for planting troughs.

Growing crops in urban areas

What most urban gardens **may lack in size**, they make up for with **opportunities**. Being able to grow **fresh fruit and vegetables** within sight of your home is **highly rewarding**, and also surprisingly **straightforward**.

Light

- Closely-packed buildings create pockets of light and shade, which you can take advantage of.
- Prune back any overhanging branches of larger trees and shrubs to allow more light into your garden.
- Walls overlooking your garden could be painted white to reflect extra light onto your crops.

Temperature

- Urban plots are sheltered and warmed by surrounding buildings, which creates milder "urban heat islands".
- The sheltered conditions allow an earlier start in spring and a long growing season.
- The milder temperatures allow you to grow tender crops, such as cucumbers.

Water

- Crops growing in containers will need frequent watering. Consider installing a water butt or an outside tap.
- Walls and fences can prevent the rain from reaching your plants, so check them regularly to see if they need watering.

Wind

- Balconies and rooftop gardens can be exposed to wind, so choose low-growing crops and support taller plants.
- Nearby buildings can channel the wind, so install windbreaks, such as trellis or wind-resistant plants.
- When positioning pots on shelves or putting up hanging baskets, ensure they cannot be blown off.

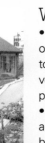

Weighty issues

- If you garden on a balcony or roof terrace, be careful not to overload it. Wet compost is very heavy and your growing plants will also gain weight.
- When putting up wall shelves and brackets for containers and baskets, be sure they are firmly attached, and will safely take the necessary weight.

5 benefits of urban gardens

- They tend to be warmer in winter, ideal for tender crops.

- They warm up quickly in spring, giving your crops an earlier start.

- The shelter from nearby buildings encourages rapid plant growth.

- An early start and a late finish gives your crops a long growing season.

- Often smaller, they are easy to maintain.

Understanding light

The amount of light in your garden plays an important role when planning what to grow. Some crops, such as tomatoes and chillies, need at least six hours of sun a day to grow well, whereas lettuces thrive in just three.

An average summer's day in England provides over 16 hours of daylight. In Scotland, a typical winter's day can give less than 6½ hours of light.

The effects of light and shade

Full sun

- Sunny sites can be very **warm**, and plants need watering often.
- **Fruits**, such as tomatoes, **ripen** more quickly in full sun.
- Most plants **flower** more **readily** in full sun, which is essential for **fruiting** crops.
- Heat can **stress** crops, leaving them prone to **disease**. Leaf crops may "bolt" (suddenly flower).

Partial sun

- East- and west-facing plots offer **a balance** of sun and shade, and suit **many crops**.
- Many **sun-loving** crops can be grown in partial sun, although **won't crop** as freely.
- You may be able to **reduce** the amount of shade in your garden by removing **shadow-forming** plants and structures.

Partial shade

- Shadier plots are **colder** and are slow to warm up in **spring**.
- Sun-loving plants grow **weak and spindly** when grown in shade.
- Most **leafy crops** prefer some shade; they can **scorch** if positioned in full sun.
- **Slugs and snails** prefer cool, damp areas, and can be a **problem** in shadier gardens.

Make a photo diary

Grab your **camera** and start noting where **sun and shade** occur in your garden **throughout** the day. This will help you to find the **brightest** spots for your crops.

10AM

12 NOON

What does full sun actually mean?

Urban plots often only have sun for part of the day. So in these conditions, full sun means direct sunlight for at least six hours a day, and for shadier areas, a minimum of three hours a day.

3PM

5PM

SUMMER Light levels are good at this time because the sun is at its highest in the sky, at least until midsummer. There is less shadow and the days are warmer and longer, which encourages plant growth.

WINTER Light levels are poor because the sun is low in the sky and the light itself is less intense. The days are also cool and short, especially in northern areas, meaning that plant growth is very slow.

Water

Water is vital for healthy crops, and since growing them in small spaces often means doing so in containers, you need to be prepared to water them often. Usefully, there are steps to take to make this easier.

- Use **larger pots**, as these dry out **less quickly**.
- Stand your pots on **drip trays** to keep the compost moist.
- **Soak plants** well before planting to encourage **rooting**.
- Be aware of the **"rain shadows"** around your garden.

Easier watering

To make watering easier, fit an outside tap, or site a water butt near to your crops. Buy a hose that will reach your plants easily, and a good reel to store it neatly. Micro-irrigation kits and seep hoses can save hours of time, and are easy to fit. Also mulch your pots to prevent evaporation.

Exposure

Being exposed to strong wind causes plants to dry out more quickly, and can scorch the leaves and damage the stems. Balconies and roof gardens are most at risk, although any plot can be affected if nearby buildings create wind tunnels. Wind can be defeated, however.

- Use trellises to **filter and slow** the wind, so it is less damaging. Trellis also offers **support to climbers**.
- Avoid solid windbreaks that cause **damaging currents** on the leeward side.
- Position new **greenhouses and sheds** to break up wind tunnels affecting your plot.
- Use **multi-layered** barriers of plants and structures to **diffuse strong winds**.
- Add low-level barriers, **like netting** or sheets of plastic, to help **low-growing** crops.
- Use **cloches** to help protect vulnerable **young plants**.

Wind-proof plants

Tougher plants that withstand and filter the wind can make an attractive feature, and can also be used to provide habitat for beneficial wildlife. Try wild roses (*Rosa*), hawthorn (*Crataegus*), and shrubby honeysuckles (*Lonicera*). Grasses also work well, swaying in a breeze.

Closer to the ground, use Mediterranean plants, such as lavender (*Lavandula*) and sage (*Salvia*). Grow them at the edges of beds to protect your leafy crops from wind scorch.

Getting to know your soil

Whether you grow them in pots, or directly in borders or raised beds, good soil is the key to healthy plants that crop well, and are more resistant to pests and diseases. By getting to know your soil, you will understand how to improve it to get the best results.

- The **ideal soil**, such as **loam** (*see right*), retains **moisture** and **nutrients** well, but drains freely.
- **Most** garden soils are rich in either **heavy clay** or **sand**.
- All soil types can be improved by adding **organic matter** to increase **drainage**, or moisture and nutrient **retention**.

Loam
This is the perfect garden soil, comprising a well-balanced mixture of clay, sand, and silt particles, and organic matter.

Clay soil
Heavy clay soil holds onto nutrients well, but drains poorly. It can be heavy to dig when wet and can bake hard in summer.

Sandy soil
Light sandy soil drains very freely, leaching moisture and nutrients. It is always worth improving it with organic matter.

Checking your soil type

Your soil type can be easily tested just by rubbing a small amount between your fingers. Clay soil, with its sticky texture, will be easy to mould into balls that will hold their shape. Sandy soils will feel gritty to the touch and won't hold together; loamy soils will feel silky and should mould into shapes fairly well.

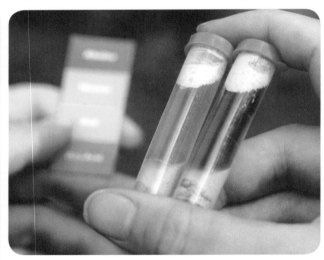

Is your soil acid or alkaline?

The pH of your soil will influence the crops you can grow, and it can be easily tested using a kit bought from garden centres. Most vegetables prefer slightly acid soil, and although soil pH can be altered, it's best to grow the crops that suit the soil you have. If your soil isn't ideal for what you want to grow, plant in pots or in a raised bed instead.

Improving your soil

Well-rotted organic matter is ideal for improving both clay and sandy soils. Rather than digging it in, however, lay it on the surface as a mulch, and allow earth worms to draw it into the soil. As they tunnel and feed, worms aerate the soil and improve its structure.

Clay soil

Clay soil is made up of very fine particles that stick together, which impedes drainage. Adding coarse organic matter physically breaks up the clay, making it lighter to dig, and improving drainage.

Recycled green waste
Garden or park waste is often available from recycling centres and local municipal authorities. This nutrient-rich compost will aerate the soil and act as a slow-release feed.

Well-rotted manure
Manure is full of degraded straw, which helps break up clay soil. It is also rich in nutrients, and acts as a slow-release feed. Only use well-rotted manure, never fresh.

Sandy soil

Sandy soil is very porous, meaning that moisture and soluble nutrients are quickly lost. Adding bulky organic matter works like a sponge, helping to retain moisture and nutrients in the soil for longer.

Home-made garden compost
Absolutely free, it acts as a slow-release feed, as well as improving the aeration and water retention of your soil. It can also be used to fill containers if mixed with soil.

Leafmould
This is excellent for increasing the water retention and organic content of light soils. It's easy to make: store wet autumn leaves in bags for two years, and it's ready to use.

Making your own garden compost

Any disease-free leafy and twiggy plant material can be added to a compost heap, which breaks down over a few months to produce a good all-round soil improver – all for free.

Adding plant material
To fill a compost bin, add leafy and twiggy material and kitchen waste in layers. Doing this will ensure good airflow.

Turning the compost bin
Continue adding material and periodically turn the heap using a fork. This adds air and encourages the composting process.

The finished compost
Compost is ready to use when it is dark and crumbly. Empty the compost out and return material that isn't fully degraded to the bin.

6 Benefits of raised beds

Raised beds are a wonderfully rich environment to grow fruit and vegetables in, and come in all shapes and sizes – essentially what you decide. What's more, they can be positioned to grab the most sun in your garden, and be conveniently situated near the kitchen door for easy harvesting.

1 Ideal for soil-less spaces

No soil – don't despair! Raised beds enable you to grow the crops of your dreams. For less hungry and smaller crops, such as lettuces and radishes, 15cm (6in) of depth is great. However, for hungrier and deep-rooted plants, such as courgettes and beetroots, aim for a minimum of 30cm (12in) depth.

2 Providing ideal growing conditions

Many gardens have problematic soil, whether heavy clay or very light and sandy. Building raised beds, and adding the perfect mix of compost and topsoil (*see pp.22–23*), will allow you to instantly start growing a whole range of exciting fruits, herbs, and vegetables.

3 Temporary growing space

If you rent your home, have building works on the horizon, or are dabbling in a bit of guerrilla gardening on a patch of unloved public space (and why not?), raised beds are ideal. They are quick, cheap, and easy to construct, and allow you to quickly start growing, even if it's just for one season.

4 Using recycled materials

The world is your oyster when it comes to using recycled materials to make raised beds. Old bricks, scaffolding boards, and metal sheets are ideal materials. Or, plant directly into used tyres or even an old paddling pool.

5 Protecting crops from pests

Compared to traditional vegetable patches, being contained areas, raised beds are much easier to protect against pests. Netting can be secured along the sides to keep birds from stealing your succulent fruit or to prevent butterflies laying eggs on your brassicas. Use chicken wire to deter larger pests, such as pigeons, cats, foxes, and deer.

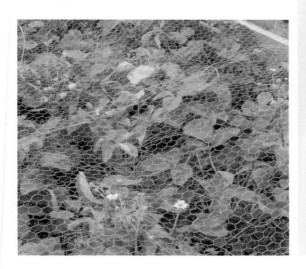

6 Giving you easier access

Making your beds no wider than 1–1.2m (3–4ft) across will make it easier for you to tend your crops without the need to tread on the soil, compacting it. The higher the bed, the less bending down you'll have to do, which can be a godsend if you have a bad back or troublesome knees.

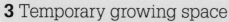

An early start

A **useful advantage** of raised beds is that they **warm up** more **quickly** in spring. This allows you to **sow and plant** out **earlier** than you could if growing your crops **directly** in the soil. An **early start** gives you **more time** to grow **crops**.

Raised beds are ideal for gardens with no soil, and can easily be sited on decks, roof terraces, and patios. Just be sure that any water that drains from the base has somewhere to go.

The perfect height

To provide adequate depth for plant roots, raised beds should provide at least 15cm (6in) of soil. However, they can be much deeper, even allowing you to grow crops with big tubers, such as potatoes. Deeper beds also have the advantage that they retain moisture better, so are less prone to drying out.

Filling your raised bed

Building a raised bed gives you the perfect opportunity to provide your plants with the ideal growing conditions, to ensure the best crops. Using the ratio below, mix the topsoil, compost, and coarse grit together in a wheelbarrow, or on a large sheet of plastic laid on the ground, before filling the bed.

45% topsoil

45% peat-free compost

10% coarse grit

Wondrous worms

Worms are an essential ally in the garden, and are vital to healthy soil. Feeding on organic matter, such as garden compost and rotting leaves, they draw it deeply into the soil, aerating it as they do so. As they feed, worms release nutrients that in turn feed your plants. Crops in raised beds will also benefit from a healthy worm population, so add some to the soil, and encourage them to stay by mulching.

Do you dig it?

The "No Dig" approach is an alternative gardening method. Not digging the soil, and disturbing it as little as possible, maintains the soil's complex structure and prevents weed seeds being brought to the surface. Rather than digging it over every year, the soil is instead mulched with well-rotted organic matter, such as garden compost. Worms then work the material into the soil.

1 Finding the best positions
By using pots, you can site them to suit your plants, whether that's basking in the sun or in the cool shade. You can also move them as the season changes to find the best positions.

5 Reasons to use containers

The advantage of growing crops in containers is that they are highly versatile. Pots allow you to provide the best conditions for your plants, and with artful positioning, they help you make best use of your space. Whenever possible, choose larger containers, as these retain water and nutrients better.

3 Planting in grow bags

Grow bags make easy, inexpensive containers. Nutrient-hungry crops, such as climbing beans, courgettes, and potatoes, need deep grow bags with rich soil and plenty of water. Grow bags for tomatoes tend to be shallower, so water them often.

4 Making use of small spaces

Some crops, such as pea shoots and round salad carrots, will grow even in small pots, allowing you to make use of the most confined spaces. With clever design ideas, you can utilize almost any area. Consider using shelves, hanging baskets, and saddlebags (*see pp.66–69*).

2 Creating an attractive feature

Be it a gorgeous series of herb pots welcoming you home with delicious scents, or quirky recycled containers full of edible flowers, producing food can be highly decorative and creative, too. Have fun designing your space!

5 Keeping your crops close to hand

What's not to love about having your dinner growing in pots right there on your patio? Freshly picked herbs and salad leaves, juicy berries, and home-grown tomatoes – nothing tastes better! You'll also save time shopping at the end of a busy day, and use zero food miles, too.

Being creative with containers

The beauty of containers is that they are so versatile. Whether sat on the ground, fixed to walls, hung, or placed on shelves, they allow you to grow crops practically anywhere.

Look **around** your plot for areas that **provide enough light** to grow plants, **choose** pots that **will fit** there, and start growing. **Larger containers** are best, but **even small** ones can **be used** to grow **certain crops**.

Tender perennial crops, such as cucamelons and figs, can be grown outside in pots over summer, then brought indoors to overwinter.

Containers in every corner

With a little imagination, and possibly some handiwork, pots help make full use of your space. Don't forget that your planters need to be easily accessible for watering and harvesting, however.

Climbing crops, such as cucumbers and beans, make good use of small spaces, as the growth is trained vertically. If well watered and fed, all can be grown in large containers.

Grouping containers together can provide a significant amount of growing space, (*see pp.132–155*). By using attractive planters, you can also create a great feature.

Windowboxes are ideal for growing smaller crops, such as lettuces, and those that trail, like strawberries. Choose colourful varieties that look as good as they taste.

Saddlebags are easy to make yourself (*see pp.66–69*) and can be hung over railings, such as on balconies. Make them big enough to fill the space you have available.

Hanging baskets make great use of vertical spaces, and can be fixed to walls, fences, and garden structures. They are ideal for trailing plants, like tumbling tomatoes.

Using shelves and growing your plants in layers is a brilliant use of a small space. They can be permanently fixed to walls, or placed on ladders as a temporary solution.

Preparing your containers

Container-grown crops **rely on you** to ensure they have adequate **food** and **water**. Keep them **content** by **preparing** their **pots** well, and using the **correct compost**.

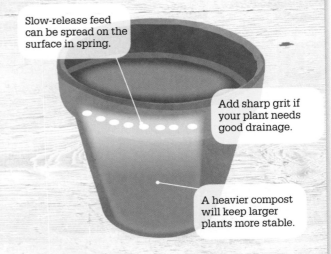

Annual crops
These growing quickly, so require a compost that is nutrient-rich and retains moisture well.

Use liquid feed for hungry growers, such as tomatoes.

Add slow-release fertilizer to feed crops all season.

Peat-free multi-purpose compost is ideal for vegetables.

MULTI-PURPOSE COMPOST retains moisture well, and is light and easy to use. However, being made from organic materials, it gradually breaks down over time.

Perennial and shrubby crops
These long-term crops need a compost that will support healthy growth for many years.

Slow-release feed can be spread on the surface in spring.

Add sharp grit if your plant needs good drainage.

A heavier compost will keep larger plants more stable.

SOIL-BASED COMPOST, such as John Innes, is heavy, and keeps potted perennials, shrubs, and trees stable. It doesn't degrade over time, and retains nutrients well.

Feeding container plants

Most composts provide enough nutrients to last 4–6 weeks, after which your crops could start to need more nutrients and fail to thrive unless you take steps to support them.

• Mix slow-release fertilizer pellets into the compost at the time of planting, which will feed your plants all season.

• Apply a liquid feed weekly to give a boost to hungry crops, such as tomatoes and courgettes.

• Spread mulch or slow-release fertilizer on the soil of plants that have been growing in pots for more than one year.

GOOD DRAINAGE

Plants need good drainage to prevent their roots becoming waterlogged, so ensure any container you use has ample holes in the bottom. If it does not, carefully make some using a drill. To stop the drainage holes becoming blocked with compost, cover them with pieces of broken pot, known as "crocks", or bits of broken-up polystyrene. Some plants need very good drainage, so mix coarse grit into their compost.

Preparing to plant up

KEEPING ROOTS COOL Metal containers are poorly insulated, allowing the compost inside to become warm, which plants don't like. Prevent this by lining the insides with bubble plastic before filling with compost, taking care not to block the drainage holes. Pierce some holes to be sure.

REUSING OLD COMPOST
If you've used multi-purpose compost to grow quick-growing crops, such as microgreens, that have only been in it for a few weeks, you could reuse it. Pick out any plant debris, add slow-release feed, and top it up with compost. Any compost used for longer than a few weeks is best discarded.

POSITIONING LARGE CONTAINERS is easiest to do before you fill them with compost.

What should I grow?

......what you like eating!

Good to eat

When **time** and **space** are limited, grow the **fruit** and **vegetables** that you find the **most delicious**, whether that's **tasty peas** or **juicy** apples. As long as you can **provide** the **right conditions**, simply grow the **crops** you **love** the most.

Suit your site

If your **garden** is **shady**, sun-loving crops like **chillies** aren't for you, but there are **loads** of **other things** you can grow **instead**. To **enjoy** the best **harvests**, choose crops that **suit** the **conditions** your garden provides (*see pp.224–241*).

Best fresh

Think about crops that are **best** eaten **fresh**, like **peas** and **sweetcorn**, or those that are **expensive** to buy. You can even grow crops you **rarely** see **sold** in shops, such as deliciously **aromatic** herbs, like **sorrel** and **sweet Cicely**.

Time wise

Choose **fast growing** crops to help **make the most** of the space you have. **Speedy** crops, such as **pea shoots**, are **ready to pick** in a matter of **weeks**, giving you time to **grow something** else **in their place**, (*see pp.50–51*).

What plants can you fit in?

Use this **guide** to **help you** decide the best **crops** for your **growing space**.

Don't **forget** to include the **places where** you can **set** pots, **hang** baskets, and **train climbing** crops **vertically**.

CROP	Planting distance (cm/in)	Height (cm/in)	Plant habit
Tomatoes – bush	30–90 (12–36)	30–120 (12–48)	Dense and bushy
Tomatoes – cordon	40–45 (16–18)	150–180 (60–72)	Upright and leafy
Sweet peppers	35–45 (14–18)	60–90 (24–36)	Dense and bushy
Chillies	35–45 (14–18)	30–90 (12–36)	Dense and bushy
Aubergines	60–75 (24–30)	60–90 (24–36)	Dense and bushy
Courgettes	90 (36)	30–45 (12–18)	Leafy and spreading
Summer squashes	90 (36)	30–45 (12–18)	Leafy and spreading
Cucumbers	45 (18)	180 (72)	Climbing or spreading
Cucamelons	30–40 (12–16)	2.5m (8ft)	Climbing or spreading
Pea shoots	2 (¾)	5–10 (2–4)	Upright and leafy
Peas	5 (2)	60–120 (24–48)	Climbing or upright
French beans	5–10 (2–4)	100–180 (39–72)	Dense and climbing
Runner beans	15 (6)	180 (72)	Dense and climbing
Broad beans	25 (10)	90–120 (36–48)	Upright and leafy
Radishes	1 (½)	15 (6)	Low and leafy
Carrots	5–10 (2–4)	15–30 (6–12)	Low and leafy
Beetroots	5–10 (2–4)	25–35 (10–14)	Low and leafy
Potatoes	30–40 (12–16)	75–90 (30–36)	Dense and bushy
Turnips	10–15 (4–6)	30–45 (12–18)	Low and leafy
Kohl rabi	25 (10)	30–45 (12–18)	Low and leafy
Florence fennel	30 (12)	60–90 (24–36)	Low and leafy
Spring onions	1 (½)	25–35 (10–14)	Low and leafy
Garlic	20 (8)	30–35 (12–14)	Upright and sparse
Leeks	15–20 (6–8)	45–60 (18–24)	Upright and leafy
Lettuce	15–35 (6–14)	15–30 (6–12)	Low and leafy
Spinach	15 (6)	30–60 (12–24)	Upright and leafy
Mustard leaves	15–30 (6–12)	15–20 (6–8)	Low and leafy
Rocket	15 (6)	15–20 (6–8)	Low and leafy
Swiss chard	20 (8)	45–60 (18–24)	Upright and leafy
Pak choi	10–25 (4–10)	30–65 (12–26)	Low and leafy
Endive	25 (10)	35–40 (14–16)	Low and leafy
Chicory	30 (12)	40–50 (16–20)	Low and leafy
Kale	60 (24)	50–90 (20–36)	Upright and leafy
Sprouting broccoli	60 (24)	90–120 (36–48)	Upright and leafy
Sweetcorn	35–45 (14–18)	150–180 (60–72)	Upright and leafy

Small space rating (see p.224)	Small pots	Large pots	Windowboxes	Hanging baskets	Raised beds
			SUITABLE FOR		
★★★		✓	Miniature	Tumblers	✓
★★★		✓			✓
★★		✓			✓
★★★	✓	✓	✓		✓
★		✓	✓		✓
★★		✓			✓
★★		✓			✓
★★★		✓			✓
★		✓		✓	✓
★★★	✓	✓	✓	✓	✓
★★		✓			✓
★★★		✓			✓
★★★		✓			✓
★		✓			✓
★★★	Baby	✓	Round	Round	✓
★★	Round	✓	Baby or round	Baby	✓
★★★	Baby	✓	Baby		✓
★		✓			✓
★★		Round	Baby		✓
★★★		✓			✓
★		✓			✓
★★	✓	✓	✓	✓	✓
★		✓	✓		✓
★★		✓			✓
★★★	✓	✓	✓	✓	✓
★★		✓			✓
★★★	✓	✓	✓		✓
★★★	✓	✓	✓	✓	✓
★★★	✓	✓	✓		✓
★★★	✓	✓		✓	✓
★★		✓	✓		✓
★★		✓	✓		✓
★★		✓	✓		✓
★		✓			✓
★		✓			✓

When growing crops for baby produce, you can sow and plant them more closely. However, keep them well watered, so they don't compete with one another.

HERBS	Planting distance (cm/in)	Height (cm/in)	Plant habit	Small space rating	SUITABLE FOR				
					Small pots	Large Pots	Window-boxes	Hanging baskets	Raised beds
French sorrel	30 (12)	30–50 (12–20)	Upright and leafy	★★★		✓			✓
Lovage	60 (24)	180 (72)	Upright and leafy	★★★		✓			✓
Parsley	15 (6)	30–90 (12–36)	Low and leafy	★★	✓	✓	✓	✓	✓
Sweet Cicely	60 (24)	100–180 (39–72)	Upright and sparse	★★★		✓			✓
Fennel	45 (18)	120–150 (48–60)	Upright and feathery	★★★		✓			✓
Borage	20 (8)	30–100 (12–39)	Low and leafy	★★★		✓	✓		✓
Sage	40 (16)	45–90 (18–36)	Leafy shrub	★★		✓	✓		✓
Lavender	50 (20)	45–120 (18–48)	Dense shrub	★★		✓	✓		✓
Rosemary	40 (16)	60–120 (24–48)	Upright shrub	★★		✓	✓		✓
Sweet basil	25 (10)	30–60 (12–24)	Low and leafy	★★★	✓	✓	✓	✓	✓
African basil	30 (12)	50–60 (20–24)	Low and leafy	★★		✓	✓	✓	✓
Mint	30 (12)	60–120 (24–48)	Upright and leafy	★★★		✓	✓		✓
French tarragon	60 (24)	60–90 (24–36)	Upright and leafy	★★★		✓	✓		✓
Chives	15 (6)	30–45 (12–18)	Upright and sparse	★★★	✓	✓	✓	✓	✓
Dill	20 (8)	60–90 (24–36)	Upright and sparse	★★★		✓	✓		✓
Pot marjoram	25 (10)	15–45 (6–18)	Low and leafy	★★★	✓	✓	✓	✓	✓
Thyme	30 (12)	5–25 (2–10)	Creeping	★★★	✓	✓	✓	✓	✓
Coriander	30 (12)	30–60 (12–24)	Low and leafy	★★★	✓	✓	✓	✓	✓

FRUIT	Planting distance (cm/in)	Height (cm/in)	Plant habit	Small space rating	Small pots	Large Pots	Window-boxes	Hanging baskets	Raised beds
Strawberries (inc. alpine types)	30–40 (12–16)	15–30 (6–12)	Low and leafy	★★	✓	✓	✓	✓	✓
Autumn raspberries	35–45 (14–18)	120–150 (48–60)	Dense and upright	★★★		✓			✓
Japanese wineberries	2.5–3.5m (8–11ft)	1.8–3m (6–10ft)	Unruly shrub, can be trained along canes and wires	★★		✓			✓
Blackberries	2.5–3.5m 8–11ft	1.8–3m (6–10ft)	Unruly shrub, can be trained along canes and wires	★★		✓			✓
Blueberries	1.5m (5ft)	90–150 (36–60)	Bushy	★		✓			✓
Apples – on dwarf rootstocks	1.8–3.6m (6–12ft)	2–3m (6–10ft)	Tree	★		✓			✓
Pear – on dwarf rootstocks	1.8–3.6m (6–12ft)	2–3m (6–10ft)	Tree	★	✓	✓			✓
Apples – trained forms	2.5–3.5m (8–11ft)	Depends on form grown	Space-saving forms	★★					✓

15 Top sun-loving crops

Some plants will need at least six hours of direct sunlight per day to produce crops that develop fully and will ripen well. If your courtyard, balcony, or roof terrace is a suntrap, these plants will thrive, giving you the sweetest tasting fruit and vegetables.

1 TOMATOES There are many exciting varieties. Try 'Green Zebra' and 'Banana Legs', which you won't find in shops.

2 COURGETTES Sow yellow and green varieties in repeated batches for masses of this versatile fruit.

3 AUBERGINES Best suited for warm climates or raising under cover, there are purple and white-fruited varieties.

4 CHILLIES Edible and decorative, the fruits develop in a stunning array of shapes, sizes, colours, and tastes.

5 SWEET PEPPERS Best in a warm spot, the brightly coloured fruits will enliven any vegetable patch.

6 STRAWBERRIES The taste of summer, grow early and late varieties to extend your harvest.

7 FENNEL The feathery leaves are almost reason enough to grow this delicious aniseed-flavoured herb.

8 BASIL As well as sweet basil, also try purple, Thai, African and cinnamon varieties for more interesting flavours.

Others to try
- Cucumbers
- Summer squashes
- French and runner beans
- Florence fennel
- Rosemary
- Raspberries
- Garlic

15 Top shade-tolerant crops

Not all plants need full sun to grow well, and some, especially leafy crops, relish a cooler, shadier position. If your growing space is north-facing, or there are surrounding trees or buildings that block out the sun for part of the day, these crops are ideal choices.

1 LETTUCES Sow little and often for an endless supply, and plant a mix of varieties for a decorative effect.

2 SWISS CHARD The variety 'Bright Lights' has vividly coloured stems that glow in the sun. It will crop into winter.

3 MUSTARD LEAVES With varied colours and textures, these spicy leaves are ideal for salads and stir-fries.

4 SPINACH Pick the leaves small and tender to use fresh in salads, or let them grow larger to enjoy them cooked.

5 AUTUMN RASPBERRIES 'Polka' produces copious amounts of huge juicy berries from late summer.

6 ALPINE STRAWBERRIES These berries are small but extremely tasty. Plant them along paths or in containers.

7 RUNNER BEANS This climbing crop bears attractive red or white flowers, and an abundance of summer beans.

8 SORREL An underused, easy-to-grow perennial herb with a delicious lemony bite. Use it in salads and soups.

Others to try
- Rocket
- Parsley
- Peas
- Radishes
- Sweet Cicely
- Mint
- Coriander

15 Top high-yielding crops

If you only have a limited amount of room to grow fruit and vegetables, it's important to choose those crops that make best use of the space they occupy by rewarding you with an abundant harvest. Those that crop over a long period are especially worthwhile.

1 FRENCH AND RUNNER BEANS These climbing beans bear purple, yellow, or green pods for many weeks.

2 ROCKET A dual-purpose crop, the peppery leaves are perfect for salads, while the flowers are sweet and spicy.

3 BEETROOTS Giving two crops in one, these are grown for their leaves and roots. 'Chioggia' has stripy flesh.

4 LETTUCES Delicious and decorative, only pick outer leaves when cropping, or enjoy a cut-and-come-again harvest.

5 RADISHES These are swift growers – sow seed every few weeks for a ready supply of crunchy, hot bites.

6 MUSTARD LEAVES This hot and spicy leaf crop can be picked over a long period, or be resown regularly.

7 COURGETTES These fleshy fruits come thick and fast in summer, more so when they are picked regularly.

8 SWISS CHARD The young fresh leaves are good for salads, while older, larger ones can be cooked like spinach.

Others to try
- Early potatoes
- Courgettes
- Spinach
- Carrots
- Microgreens
- Perpetual strawberries
- Kai lan

15 Top quick-growing crops

Just as space is limited in the garden, so too is time, and it's important to take full advantage of the growing season. These are some of the quickest vegetables to grow, swiftly providing pickings from your plot, then making way, ready for you to sow more vegetables.

1 PEA SHOOTS Ready to pick in just 3 weeks, the crisp shoots are fresh and succulent. Perfect for many salads.

2 MICROGREENS Taking 3–5 weeks, these intensely flavoursome mini leaves can be grown from spare seeds.

3 RADISHES Taking 4–6 weeks, sow these fiery roots in regular batches for a constant supply throughout summer.

4 ROCKET Mature leaves are ready to eat in 4–5 weeks, and you can also use the thinnings as microgreens.

5 PAK CHOI Within 6–8 weeks, these fresh and succulent oriental greens can be eaten raw or used in stir-fries.

6 COURGETTES These start bearing fruits within 8–10 weeks. The male flowers can also be picked and eaten.

7 CARROTS Ready to harvest within 8–10 weeks, try mini round 'Paris Market' or multi-coloured 'Harlequin'.

8 KAI LAN Pick after 8–10 weeks, and let the stem resprout. It looks like a cross between asparagus and broccoli.

Others to try
- Swiss chard
- Beetroots
- Kohl rabi
- Lettuces
- French and runner beans
- Florence fennel
- Early potatoes

15 Top easy-care crops

Some vegetables are prima donnas, demanding attention throughout their growing season. Others however, once planted, grow happily away on their own, just waiting for you to harvest when the crop ripens. If growing them in pots, don't forget to water though!

1 RUNNER BEANS Simply plant these robust climbers at the base of a cane and look forward to a good harvest.

2 STRAWBERRIES Feed in spring, cut off any runners, and these plants will crop for several weeks to come.

3 AUTUMN RASPBERRIES Once planted, mulch in spring, enjoy the fruit, then remove all stems in late winter.

4 COURGETTES Always water well, and feed if fruiting starts to flag. Pick courgettes small to encourage fruiting.

5 KOHLRABI Sow seeds in batches in spring and summer, then watch the unusual-looking crop develop.

6 PEA SHOOTS Soak dried peas overnight, sow, and 3 weeks later pick the shoots once large enough to use.

7 SPROUTING BROCCOLI Slow but easy to grow, sow in spring, plant out in summer, then crop next spring.

8 SWISS CHARD This hardy crop will grow through winter, when you can harvest the leaves as you need them.

Others to try
- Beetroots
- Lettuces
- Carrots
- Mustard leaves
- Mint
- Sorrel
- Sweet Cicely

15 Top shallow-rooted crops

Shallow-rooted vegetables are a godsend for growing on balconies, windowsills, and rooftops, where the quantity of soil, and especially its weight, is a serious consideration. All of these crops can be grown in a mere 15cm (6in) of soil when kept well watered.

1 LETTUCES Harvest the plants as a cut-and-come-again crop, or as mature heads. Sow seed in regular batches.

2 RADISHES Small round varieties, such as 'Cherry Belle', are perfect for growing in pots and shallow beds.

3 FLORENCE FENNEL Decorative and tasty, plant them 30cm (12in) apart to allow decent sized bulbs to develop.

4 CHIVES Both the stems and flowers of this useful perennial herb are edible. Divide congested plants in spring.

5 MUSTARD LEAVES Try growing 'Green in Snow', 'Red Giant' and 'Osaka Purple' for a mix of tastes.

6 FRENCH AND RUNNER BEANS Water well and harvest regularly to grow beans well on shallower soils.

7 ALPINE STRAWBERRIES Ideal to plant along the edges of beds, these small berries are very sweet and tasty.

8 TOMATOES At home in shallow beds and growing bags, keep plants well watered and fed during summer.

Others to try
- Peas
- Garlic
- Swiss chard
- Marigolds
- Nasturtiums
- Mint
- Sage

Making the most of your growing space

Once you have identified your growing space, the next step is to use it as productively as possible. This means squeezing in as many crops as you can, encouraging them to produce the biggest harvest possible, and ensuring the space is bountifully planted all season.

The **best place** to grow crops is in a **bed**, ideally a **raised** one that can be **filled** with **fertile soil**, and **tended** at the **sides**, allowing **crops** to be **closely packed**. Dividing it into **equal** areas helps you **allocate** space to **crops** with **little waste**.

Container growing

EVEN SMALL PLOTS produce bountiful crops, because fruit and vegetables can be grown just as intensively in containers as when planted in beds. Even if you don't have a single large area to devote to your crops, the growing space offered by several containers can add up significantly, as shown here. The nine containers shown on the left (*see also pp.132–155*) provide exactly the same growing space as the bed above. However, they have the advantage that you can position them around your plot, using every spot available.

Raising crops in pots to plant out when existing ones are harvested means your plot is always productive. Plan your sowing and planting in advance (see pp.224—241).

Harvesting crops all season

CROPS GROW AND MATURE at different rates, which helps you use your space and the growing season efficiently. Quick-growing crops provide several harvests in a single season, and can be planted to make use of the space around those that are slower (*see pp.50–51*). Low-growers, such as lettuces, can be planted beneath taller crops, such as sweetcorn. You need never waste an inch!

Extending the growing season

Seeds and plants grow quicker in warmer conditions, and there are simple ways to provide them. This will give the plants an earlier start, prolong the season, and increase your harvest.

- **Warming** the soil enables you to **sow** seeds **outside** earlier.
- Sow seeds **under cover** to give plants a **head start** in spring.
- **Cloches** and covers encourage **growth**, and **allow plants** to **crop for longer**.

The seed of most crops can be sown in pots on a bright windowsill. This is ideal for those that need a long season, such as chillies.

Beating the chill

In most cases, extending the season is about eating into autumn and winter by trapping warmth and protecting your plants from cold. Even tender crops can last into autumn with a little help.

Covering your soil for a few weeks in late winter with sheets of black plastic warms the soil, allowing you to sow seeds directly outside sooner. This is ideal for raised beds.

Protecting plants in spring and autumn from frost means they develop sooner, and continue cropping for longer. Crop is pots can also be brought indoors to keep them going.

Cold frames are easy to make yourself, and ideal for raising plants. They offer frost protection, so can be used to grow crops, such as Swiss chard, through the winter.

Covering plants with cloches in spring guards against frost and encourages growth. Cloches can also be used to protect winter crops, such as endive and chicory.

Mini-greenhouses provide the perfect growing conditions for warmth-loving plants, like tomatoes, peppers, and aubergines. Here they will crop sooner, better, and for longer.

Harvesting crops regularly lengthens the season by encouraging plants to replace the leaves and fruits they have lost. Of course, this doesn't apply to root crops!

Preparing your soil

Good soil is essential for producing a healthy harvest, and time spent preparing it before planting will be well rewarded. New beds can be filled with the best mix possible (*see p.23*). With existing beds, however, you need to make the most of what's already there.

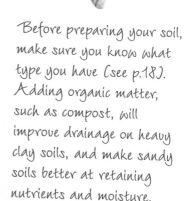

Before preparing your soil, make sure you know what type you have (see p.18). Adding organic matter, such as compost, will improve drainage on heavy clay soils, and make sandy soils better at retaining nutrients and moisture.

Giving your soil a makeover

When growing crops in a raised bed, you can employ the "no dig" approach (*see p.23*). Using this technique, well-rotted organic matter, such as garden compost or manure, is applied to the surface and left for the worms to incorporate naturally into the soil. The advantage is that the soil structure isn't damaged by digging, and the mulch can be applied around any existing crops. However, the worms don't do all the work for you, and there are further steps to improving your soil.

1 Start by weeding the soil thoroughly, being sure to remove any perennial ones completely (*see pp.246–247*). Weed roots should not be composted.

2 Water the soil well, then starting at one end of the bed, cover the surface with a deep mulch of organic matter, 10cm (4in) thick. Don't dig it in.

3 If the bed is going to remain empty in autumn and winter, sow a green manure, such as red clover (*above*), which can be dug into the soil in spring.

Busy soil is best

Soil is a living material, and the more crops you grow, the better it becomes over time. Plant roots help to break up soil, improving its drainage and aeration, and attract beneficial soil organisms, such as fungi and bacteria. Help your soil by growing lots of crops.

Sowing seeds

Growing your own vegetables from seed is especially satisfying, as it allows you to nurture your plants from the very beginning. It is easy to do in most cases, and has many practical advantages. Perennial crops and soft fruit are best grown from plants, however.

Sowing **crops from seed** allows **you** to **grow** the **widest range possible**, including **unusual varieties** you **won't see** in **shops**. It also **enables** you to grow **lots of plants** very **cheaply**. And many crops can **only be** grown from **seed**.

Seeds in outdoor pots

Seeds can be sown directly into pots outside in a similar way as in a bed. Fill the container with compost and water it well. Once it has drained, either make drills in the compost surface, or sow seeds onto the surface and cover them with more compost. Water the seeds then wait.

Sowing seeds outdoors

The easiest way to sow seeds is directly where they are to grow outside. Hardy seeds can be sown while the weather is still frosty if covered with fleece. For tender crops, wait until the last frost has passed.

1 When sowing into a raised bed, prepare the soil first by removing any weeds and stones. Rake the surface level, and break up any clumps to leave a fine crumb.

2 Using string, mark out where the seeds will be sown. Then, make drills (shallow grooves), using a dibber or trowel to the planting depth given on the seed packet.

3 Small seeds should be thinly sown along the drill – larger ones can be placed individually. Refer to the seed packet for the correct planting distances.

4 Cover the seeds over with soil and water them in gently using a can with a fine rose fitted. Once the seedlings emerge, thin them out to the recommended spacings.

Sowing under cover

Sowing seeds indoors gives you an earlier start but you will need somewhere to grow the seedlings on under cover.

1 Fill small pots or trays with multi-purpose compost, just below the rim. Water well and leave it to drain. Sow seeds lightly onto the compost and cover with more compost to the depth given on the seed packet.

2 Cover the seeds with a clear plastic bag to help retain moisture and place them somewhere warm and light. Check daily, and when seedlings appear, remove the plastic bag. Keep them moist as the seedlings grow.

3 Once the seedlings have two pairs of leaves, transplant them into trays, spacing them out with room to grow, or into individual pots. Alternatively, thin the seedlings out in their first tray.

4 Grow the seedlings on under cover. When they are large enough, or the risk of frost has passed, acclimatize them to life outside. Put them outside by day, inside at night, for ten days.

Sowing seeds in succession

Most seeds are sown from spring to late summer.
Sow all types of crops successionally, in small frequent
batches, for constant harvests in summer and autumn.

1 Quick- growing crops that mature a few weeks after sowing are ideal for successional sowing, and include pea shoots, radishes (*left*) and microgreens. These can be sown directly into your bed or in containers. Sow the seeds as directed by the packet instructions.

2 The aim is to promote rapid growth so the plants can soon be harvested. To do this, thin the seedlings so those remaining have space to grow, and don't have to compete for moisture and nutrients. Keep them well watered and fed, and watch out for pests.

3 Harvest the crops as soon as they reach a usable size, freeing up space in your bed or container. Refresh the soil by removing any plant debris, and lightly fork it. You can sow a new batch of radish or other seeds, repeating this process as long as the season lasts.

Crop rotation

In a traditional vegetable plot, you should not grow the same crops in the same area year after year. Doing so depletes the soil of the nutrients that crop requires, and also risks attracting specific pests and diseases that attack it.

Most raised beds are too small to support effective crop rotation, as the plants grow so closely together. Instead, clear plant debris to prevent diseases, control pests, and feed the soil each year.

If crops in your raised bed are attacked by tricky soil–borne diseases, such as clubroot (see p.244), consider replacing the soil completely.

Growing crops between crops

Otherwise known as "intercropping", this approach allows you to make use of the temporary spaces around and between crops that are tall and airy or slow-growing.

Taller crops, such as **sweetcorn**, leave **useful space** at their **base**, which you can **use** for **low-growers**, such as **beetroots**. **Likewise**, use any **gaps** around **slower** crops, like **sprouting broccoli**, to grow **speedier** vegetables, such as **radishes**.

Crop guide

- Tall crops: Sweetcorn, kale, and sprouting broccoli
- Low-growing crops: Radishes, courgettes, squashes, and carrots
- Slow-growing crops: Kale, sprouting broccoli, sweetcorn, and peppers
- Speedy crops: Pea shoots, radishes, baby carrots, microgreens, and rocket

Slow-growing and tall, sweetcorn can be intercropped.

Beetroots can be harvested young in a matter of weeks.

Feeding and watering

To reap the largest harvest possible from containers and raised beds, it is essential to water and feed your crops well. Keep them nourished and they will nourish you in return.

Feeding your crops

All fruit and vegetables require regular feeding as they develop, but it is important to use the correct type of fertilizer for the crops you are growing.

1 Liquid feeds provide an instant boost to your crops. It is short-lived, however, so you need to apply it regularly, usually weekly.

2 Mulching with compost is ideal for slow-growing and perennial crops, as it provides nutrients slowly and over a long period.

3 Leaf crops, such as Swiss chard and lettuces, require plenty of nitrogen to grow strongly. Feed using a balanced liquid fertilizer.

4 Fruiting crops, like courgettes, need potash to flower and fruit well. Feed them using liquid tomato feed, which is rich in potash.

Effective watering

Even though they may get rained on, your crops rely on you for water, especially those in containers.

1 Water seedlings using a can with a fine rose fitted to it to prevent damaging or washing them away.

2 Direct the water at the base of older plants so it soaks down to the roots. Avoid wetting the leaves.

3 Insert funnels made from cut-off plastic bottles to help water thirsty crops more thoroughly.

4 Conserve moisture in the soil by mulching the surface around plants. This reduces evaporation.

Micro-irrigation kits

If you have lots of containers, consider installing a simple micro-irrigation system connected to a timer. You can lay seep hoses on raised beds, connected to a timer, that will water your crops automatically.

Beneficial insects

All fruiting crops, such as courgettes and strawberries, need insects to pollinate their flowers before they can produce their fruit. Attracting pollinators into your garden by planting nectar-rich flowers will help to increase your harvest. Some pollinators are also predatory, and will help to control pests, including aphids.

Plants for pollinators

• Pollinating insects prefer simple, single flowers that they can easily access. Avoid those with fussy double blooms.
• To attract insects throughout the growing season, plant a menu of flowers that lasts from spring to autumn.
• Include spring-flowering bulbs and blossom-rich trees, summer herbs, and autumn perennials.

Lavender

California poppies

Fennel

Hollyhocks

Love-in-a-mist

Apple blossom

Making use of garden leftovers

- When harvesting your crops, don't be in a hurry to tidy up straight away. The flowers of many herbs and vegetables are loved by pollinating insects.
- Carrots and parsnips are biennial, but are normally pulled before they flower. However, bees love their blooms, so leave some in to flower next year.
- Mustard leaf bears yellow flowers if not cropped, which attract pollinators, and are edible.

Borage

Cornflowers

Crocus

Giant hyssop

Insect allies

By creating areas for insects, such as ladybirds and lacewings, to overwinter, they will be on-hand in spring to control your pests and pollinate your crops.

Bees Wild bees hibernate in holes in the ground and in trees, although you can also help by providing a "bee hotel". Feeding on nectar and pollen during summer, they are vital crop pollinators.

Hoverflies

Resembling wasps, these are doubly beneficial in the garden. Adults pollinate flowers and the larvae avidly feed on aphids.

Butterflies and moths

These pollinate flowers and are a welcome sight in the garden. They also attract beneficial birds that feed on the caterpillars.

Watch and learn

Whether you're in a nursery, or visiting a garden, take note of the plants that pollinators feed on. They will guide you to the best plants to grow. Buddleja bushes are always swathed in butterflies, and borage seems to be bee heaven.

Companion planting

Controlling damaging pests is essential to growing the biggest harvest, and there are certain plants that do some of the work for you.

While **pests flock** to **certain** plants, they **steer clear** of **others**. Grow **pest magnets away** from your crops as **a cunning lure**, and **use** those they **hate** as a **barrier**. You can also **grow plants** to attract **pest predators**.

Your growing allies

Grow these plants in your beds and containers to protect your crops from pests. All except poached egg plant are also edible, doubling their value.

POT MARIGOLDS These edible flowers attract aphid-eating hoverflies.

CHIVES Their piquant onion scent helps prevent carrot flies finding your crop.

POACHED EGG PLANT This annual attracts hoverflies that avidly feed on aphids. Sow it directly at the edge of your beds or grow it in containers placed near your crops.

GARLIC Grow carrots next to garlic to mask their scent from pesky carrot flies.

NASTURTIUMS Grow these to lure aphids away from your vulnerable crops.

THYME Plant this scented herb near your crops to help fend off aphid attacks.

FRENCH MARIGOLDS Use these pungent plants to help ward off whitefly.

SWEET BASIL Plant this herb alongside tomatoes to help repel aphid attack.

MINT Plant pots of scented mint near your beds and containers to deter aphids.

SMALL-SPACE PROJECTS

Balcony planter

Hanging a planter on railings makes great use of space on a balcony. Fill it with trailing crops, like tumbling tomatoes.

Materials

Planter
Bubble plastic
Multi-purpose
compost
Liquid tomato feed

Plants

Tumbling tomatoes
Pinks

Find a sturdy planter with strong hooks and hang it facing on to your balcony so you can enjoy the display, care for your plants, and harvest the fruits easily.

1 If you're using a metal container, line it with a piece of bubble plastic to prevent the roots heating up in hot sun. Make holes in the wrap so the planter drains freely.

2 Fill the container with multi-purpose compost, finishing 5cm (2in) below the rim to allow space for easier watering.

3 Arrange your plants and plant them, firming them in with more compost as required. Water them in thoroughly.

Care Advice

Deadheading Pick off dead flowerheads on pinks to keep them blooming throughout the summer.

Ripening At the end of the season, add green tomatoes to a fruit bowl with apples and bananas to help them ripen, or make chutney.

4 Keep the plants well watered, even in rainy spells. Begin feeding the tomato plant with liquid tomato feed weekly as soon as the first flowers begin to appear.

5 Add edible pinks to salads and pick the tomatoes when they are fully ripe, richly coloured, with a hint of softness.

Strawberry colander

Shop-bought strawberries never taste as good as those you pick yourself, and here is a way to grow them with style in a small space – by using a retro colander as a hanging basket.

Materials

Vintage or retro-style metal colander
Hanging basket bracket
Hanging basket chains
Multi-purpose compost
Bubble plastic
Scissors
Watering can

Plants

5 x strawberry plants

Combine summer-fruiting and perennial strawberry varieties (see p.233) for the longest crop, lasting from midsummer to autumn. Pick the berries when firm and bright red.

2 Measure out the bubble plastic to fit the container and don't forget to put holes in it to let water drain through. Waterlogged plants will quickly begin to die off.

3 Smooth out the bumps and ridges to allow maximum room for compost. This is a restricted space and you need to make use of every bit of it when you plant up.

1 Look for a good-sized metal colander with plenty of room in it. The drainage holes make it ideal as a planter but it will need insulating to protect the roots from overheating.

4 Half fill the colander with compost and position the strawberries evenly on the base so that they will sit about 3 cm (1¼in) below the top of the container.

5 Remove the pots. If you find the roots have become pot-bound, tease them out with your fingers before planting to help them grow out naturally into the fresh compost.

6 Fill in the gaps around the plants with compost and firm it in well, finishing the layer about 2.5cm (1in) below the rim of the colander to allow space for watering.

7 Give the plants a really good soak, and leave the colander on the ground until all the water has been absorbed. Add more compost if it has settled and left gaps between plants.

Others to try

Aromatic trailing and bushy herbs, such as oregano and basil, would be ideal to grow instead of strawberries.

Tumbling tomatoes make good hanging displays, but use just one plant per colander and water without fail every day.

8 Space the hanging basket chains evenly and attach them by clipping them to the holes in the colander. If using summer-fruiting strawberries, hang them in full sun.

9 Even if it pours with rain, little will reach the compost, so water your plants regularly. Feed weekly once in flower using a liquid tomato fertilizer to encourage fruiting.

Care Advice

Lifespan Strawberries are perennials and will bear some fruit in their first year, but crop better in the second and third.

Runners After fruiting, plants put out runners to make new plants. Snip them off to conserve the plants' energy.

Balcony saddlebags

Hanging a fabric saddlebag over a balustrade will double your growing space with crops on both sides of the rail.

Materials

Sturdy fabric, roughly 1x1.2m (3 x4ft) per saddlebag	Hammer
	Scissors
Tape measure	Chalk pencil
Heavy-duty rivet kit	Hanging basket liner
Ruler	Water-retaining gel
	Multi-purpose compost

Plants

Tomato 'Bitonto'	Swiss chard
Tumbling tomatoes	Sorrel
Strawberries	Rocket
Basil (green and purple)	Red giant mustard leaf
Oregano	Pot Marigolds
Mint	Cornflowers

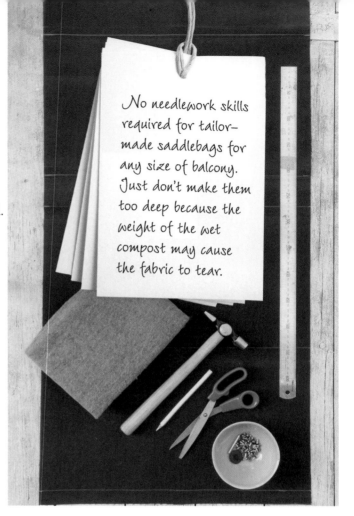

No needlework skills required for tailor-made saddlebags for any size of balcony. Just don't make them too deep because the weight of the wet compost may cause the fabric to tear.

1 Cut out the cloth to size and hem the short sides by folding in 2cm (¾in) of fabric three times and hammering in rivets, 10cm (4in) apart.

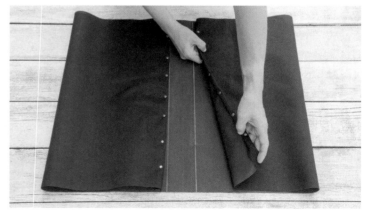

2 Leave 6cm (2½in) clear at each end. Draw two lines in the centre of the cloth to accommodate the width of your railing and allow the bags to hang, then bring the riveted ends up to the lines.

3 Turn the cloth to work on the long sides. Fold over 3cm (1¼in) of fabric twice along each of the long sides to make seams and create the bags. Rivet them in place.

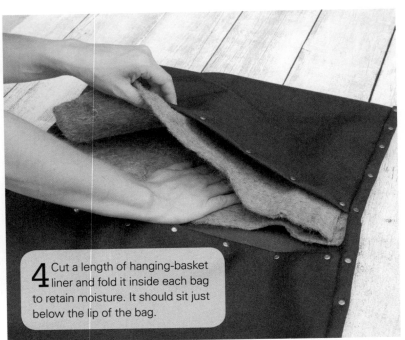

4 Cut a length of hanging-basket liner and fold it inside each bag to retain moisture. It should sit just below the lip of the bag.

5 For an extra boost to moisture retention, mix 5g (¼oz) of water-retaining gel into 5 litres (1 gallon) of multi-purpose compost before you use it to fill the bags.

6 Fill the bags, pushing the compost down into the corners to make use of all the space. Leave room at the top to accommodate your plants.

7 Hang the bags on the rail. Plant sun-loving crops and flowers on the outside and shade-tolerant plants facing inwards.

8 Firm in the plants with more compost and water them well. Keep watering throughout the season, even if it rains.

Planting combinations

Think of your saddlebags as miniature cottage gardens - a traditional mix of vegetables, fruit, and flowers that complement each other perfectly.

Marigolds and verbena add a splash of colour to this saddlebag, planted with zesty French sorrel.

Salad bag has mustard leaves and Swiss chard on the inside, with a tumbling tomato out front.

Mediterranean bag features a dwarf bush tomato, purple and green basil, and oregano.

Strawberries do best on the sunny side with a cluster of marigolds. Cornflowers and mint form a backdrop.

Care Advice

Topping up Keep the bags topped up with compost if any gets washed away, to keep the weight of each pocket even.

Tidy up Remove damaged or dying foliage and deadhead flowering plants to encourage them to bloom repeatedly.

Corn oil drum

Sun-loving sweetcorn needs a hot summer to do well.
It grows tall, so pick a deep roomy container – an oil
drum is ideal – and place it in a warm, sunny spot.

Materials

A large container at least
40cm (16in) in diameter with
drainage holes in the bottom
Multi-purpose compost

Liquid fertilizer
Watering can

Plants and seeds

Small sweetcorn plants
(bought or grown indoors
from seed)
Beetroot seeds

Sweetcorn is slow
growing and casts
little shade, which
makes it a great
candidate for
intercropping.
Try beetroot, lettuce,
rocket, parsley, or
mustard leaves.

2 Space the plants evenly in a block rather than in a row.
This will help wind pollination between the male and
female flowers, which is essential for kernels to form.

1 You can grow sweetcorn from seed indoors from mid-
spring onwards, or buy young plants. Plant out in a
sheltered spot in full sun, when danger of frost has passed.

Care Advice

Planting Sweetcorn dislikes root disturbance so don't let
young plants become too big before you plant them out.

Harvesting Most plants produce one or two cobs in
August or September. Pull apart the leaves to check for
pale yellow kernels, then twist the ripe cob off at its base.

3 Water the plants in well and continue to keep the drum well watered and free of weeds. Remove any weak or failing plants to create more space if need be.

4 Thinly scatter beetroot seeds (or seeds for fast-growing salads or herbs) between the corn. When seedlings appear, thin them out to their correct planting distances.

5 After 4–6 weeks, the sturdy plants will be depleting the nutrients in the compost. Feed them once a week with a liquid fertilizer to boost crop production.

6 Pick some of the earthy young beetroot leaves for salads. When the roots are ready to harvest a few weeks later, pull them out gently to avoid disturbing the corn.

7 For the sweetest cobs, pick them as soon as their silky tassels start to turn brown and eat them the same day. If cobs are left too long, their sugars turns to starch.

Carrot oil drum

Sow seeds thinly in multi-purpose compost in rows or circles. Planting your crop high up may help to protect it from carrot fly, which fly close to the ground.

Lightly cover the seeds with compost and water them in thoroughly with a watering can and rose. Keep the growing plants well watered.

Thin out baby carrots regularly to eat raw in salads and make room for the full-sized carrots to develop. You can eat the carrot tops too – they taste a bit like parsley.

When you can't grow out....
Go upwards!

Your **ground space** may be **limited**, but by growing **crops vertically**, you can **double**, or even **triple**, the **area** you have. Instead of placing a **raised bed** at the base of this fence (*right*), **lean-to shelves** provide **far more** space. Growing **climbing crops** up supports also maximizes **space efficiency**. Requiring the same amount of soil as a **few lettuces**, you could enjoy crops like **runner beans** that you can **harvest all summer**.

Cucumber trellis

This unusual cucumber needs little space to produce garlands of globes that taste as good as they look. For a bumper crop, choose a warm, sheltered spot.

Materials

A large container, at least 30cm (12in) in diameter
Multi-purpose compost
Slow-release fertilizer
3 x bamboo canes
Garden twine

Watering can
Liquid tomato fertilizer
Bubble plastic

Plants

Cucumber 'Crystal Apple'
(Grown from seed or bought as a small plant)

'Crystal Apple' may look unusual but its has a similar taste and texture to other cucumbers. Its advantage is that it grows well outdoors. You could also use ridge varieties.

1 Fill a large container with multi-purpose compost and mix in some slow-release fertilizer to feed the plant. If you are using a metal container, line it with bubble plastic (*see p.29*).

2 Push the bamboo canes into the compost and tie them together at the top to form a wigwam. Wind string around it from bottom to top for the cucumber to climb up.

3 Either grow your own cucumber plant from seed, sown individually in pots indoors mid-spring, or buy a plant. Harden it off and plant it out after the last frost.

4 Firm the plant into the compost and water it in well. Guide the growing tips onto the string to help the plant put out tendrils and climb the wigwam.

5 Water regularly and feed weekly with tomato fertilizer once the first flowers appear. Harvest the cucumbers as soon as they are ripe and large enough to use.

Care Advice

Watering Cucumbers are thirsty plants and should be kept moist at all times.

Harvesting Pick the fruits as soon as they are ready to ensure a constant supply. Each plant will produce up to a dozen fruits during summer.

Ladder shelves

These decorative shelves, filled with vibrant flowers and crops, are a perfect way to create valuable growing space on your patio.

Materials

2 x wooden ladders	Multi-purpose compost
3 x scaffolding boards	Liquid plant feed
Approximately 20 pots	

Plants and seeds

Tumbling tomatoes	Lettuce
Cucamelon	Strawberries
Purple basil	Chillies
Pot marigolds	Mint
Sweet Williams	Thyme
Violas	Mustard leaf

Try reclamation yards and recycling centres for ladders and planks, and unusual containers in all sizes and colours. Paint ladders and shelves to fit your garden colour scheme.

1 Place the ladders on a firm surface, facing each other, and in a sunny and sheltered spot. Evenly position the scaffolding boards to sit securely on the ladder rungs.

2 Fill a container with compost and use a dibber to make evenly spaced holes for larger seeds, like nasturtiums. Cover them over with compost and water in well.

3 To sow fine seeds, spread them over the surface of moist compost and cover them to the depth given on the packet. Keep them moist and thin once germinated.

4 Plant out young plants or potted herbs after the last frost. Release the plant gently, surround the root ball with extra compost in a larger pot, and firm it in. Water well.

SOWING MICROGREENS

Microgreens are a quick and delicious crop to grow. Try all manner of seeds for these tiny, intense leaves, such as basil, mustard leaves, kales, and rocket. Once cropped, replace with another sowing of seeds. By repeatedly sowing every few weeks, you'll have these tasty leaves all summer long.

Caring for your plants

Continually deadhead violas, marigolds, and Sweet Williams so they carry on flowering all summer.

Feed tomatoes with a liquid high-potash tomato fertilizer each week once the first flowers have appeared.

Pinch out the growing tips of the basil plants to encourage new sideshoots and strong, bushy growth.

5 Water the plants even when it rains as some of the lower pots will be in a rain shadow.

Easy lean-to shelves

Shelves are a great way to make use of sunny walls for growing crops in pots. Simple lean-to shelves that rest against the wall are especially simple to install.

Materials

Lean-to ladder kit
10–15 assorted pots
Multi-purpose compost
Power drill
Screwdriver and screws
Rawl plugs

Plants and seeds

Thyme, basil, and chives
Strawberries
Chillies
Carrot, beetroot, and lettuce seeds
Plants with edible flowers

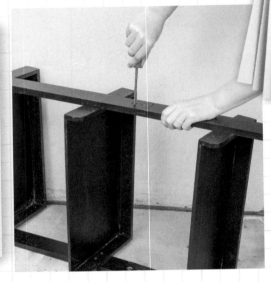

1 Choose a kit that fits neatly into the space available and make sure that it is the type that leans against the wall. Follow the instructions to assemble it.

2 Site the shelves against a sunny wall, making sure the base is on level ground, and is stable, with both sides resting flat against the wall. Fix it securely to the wall.

Care Advice

Watering To ensure larger containers don't become too heavy for their shelves when wet, place them on the ground when watering them.

Feeding Feed weekly with a liquid fertilizer. Use a balanced feed for leafy crops and tomato fertilizer for fruiting plants.

3 Ensure the pots you are using have drainage holes. If they don't, carefully make some.

SHELF LIFE
Use your own judgment, but it is usually best to put heavier plants nearer the bottom and smaller, trailing plants closer to the top of the shelves.

4 Seeds of many crops, such as carrot, can be sown directly into containers. Sprinkle the seeds finely over the compost, cover them lightly, and water in well.

5 Keep the seeds moist until they germinate, then thin the seedlings out to leave the strongest plants. Continue to thin, leaving the rest to grow on until they are harvested.

6 Pot on herbs and flowers bought as young plants into containers filled with compost. Keep the neck of the plant at the same level as it was in its pot, and firm it in.

7 Before you place your pots on the shelves, water them well. This will prevent water and soil dripping onto the plants below. If you want to keep the shelves clean, continue to put your smaller pots on the ground each time you water them.

8 Turn the containers regularly to allow each side to face the sun and help the plants to grow straight. Check crops regularly to see if they are ready to be pulled or picked.

9 Fast-growing leafy crops, such as herbs and salad leaves, can soon outgrow their allotted space on the shelves, so harvest them regularly. This will keep them cropping, too.

10 Plants that appreciate the warmth and shelter provided by a wall are ideal for shelf life. Chillies are a great choice; they will flower and fruit continually so pick them regularly and dry them for winter use. Other good plants for a low shelf include blueberries, sweet peppers, and dwarf bush tomatoes.

11 Siting trailing fruits, such as strawberries, high up on the ladder enhances this attractive feature. Growing strawberries above ground also keeps the fruits clean and away from pests, although check your shelves regularly for climbing slugs and snails. Mix in potted pinks and marigolds for a potager effect.

Bicycle wheel trellis

Pinned onto a sunny wall or fence, old bicycle wheels create a clever and creative trellis. The spokes are ideal for cucumber tendrils to cling to and climb.

Materials

3 x bicycle wheels
3 x large-headed long nails
 U-shaped metal pins
Large container
Small cane
Soft string

Hammer
Multi-purpose compost
Liquid tomato feed

Plants

1 x Climbing cucumber
(Raise from seed or buy.)

Choose any ridge variety of cucumber, as these are specially selected for growing outdoors. Those with smaller fruits, such as 'Burpless Tasty Green', are especially productive.

1 Find a warm, sheltered spot next to a sturdy fence or wall and experiment with different arrangements of wheels to allow height and space for the plant to climb.

2 Hammer a long nail with a large head through the hub of each wheel. Tack extra fixing pins over some of the spokes that lie flat against the fence.

Care Advice

Pinching out the growing tip of the plant as soon as it reaches the top of your trellis will encourage sideshoots and bushy growth across the wheels.

Powdery mildew is a white powdery coating that appears on leaves, often when a plant is underwatered. Remove damaged leaves as soon as you spot them.

3 Position the wheels so that they overlap a little and provide full support to your plant. Ensure they cannot turn in the wind, which could damage the plant stems.

4 Wait until all risk of frost has passed before planting out. Keep the compost at the same level as the neck of the plant to avoid neck rot. Firm the plant in and water it well.

5 A small bamboo cane will support the plant and help it to reach the trellis. Keep the plant watered, and protect it from pests, such as slugs, which feast on young growth.

6 As soon as the plant reaches its first wheel, tie it in loosely with soft string – then watch it grow. It will put out tendrils and climb the trellis rapidly on its own.

7 Remember to keep watering, even during wet spells. Once the first flowers appear, feed the plant weekly with a liquid tomato fertilizer to encourage a larger harvest.

8 Cucumbers mature fast and are best picked when they are about 20–25cm (8–10in) long and the skin is tender. Harvesting regularly helps to keep the plant producing fruit.

OTHER CLIMBERS

Any crop that puts out tendrils should adapt well to a bicycle trellis. Try planting one or two sugar snap pea plants in a wide container, after the last frost, and support them with twiggy sticks until they reach the first wheel. They may need a bit of training, so wind them gently round the spokes until they begin to cling. Water well and protect them from slugs and snails.

Potted bean arch

Easy-to-grow climbing beans reach dizzy heights.
Use them to frame a doorway with their pretty flowers,
and enjoy a non-stop supply of beans all summer.

*Try growing
French, runner,
and Borlotti beans
together for a
stunning display.
Red, pink, and white
flowers are followed
by yellow, purple,
red, and green beans.*

Materials

2 x matching containers, at
least 1m (3ft) long, 30cm (1ft)
wide, and 45cm (18in) deep.
10 x wooden poles or canes,
1.8–2.5m (6–8ft) long.
Multi-purpose compost

Plastic ties or garden twine
Liquid fertilizer
Watering can

Plants

Borlotti beans:
'Lingua di Fuoco 2'

French beans:
'Cobra'
'Cosse de Violette'

Runner beans:
'St. George'
'White Lady'

2 Insert four poles close to the inside edge of each planter,
leaning them towards the centre so they cross over each
other, forming an arch. Tie them in place with string or ties.

1 Beans do best in a sunny, sheltered position but will also
grow in semi-shade. Place the containers on each side
of a doorway or beside a path, and fill them with compost.

Care Advice

Pinch out the growing tips of your beans when they
reach the top of the poles to encourage sideshoots.

Keep picking because while there are still flowers on
your runner beans there will be more beans to come.
Look out for tough old beans hidden among the leaves,
and remove them before they stop the plants fruiting.

3 Beans often reach 2.5m (8ft) in height and need a strong support. Add a horizontal pole to strengthen the arch, tying it in to the vertical poles where they cross.

4 Tie in a second horizontal pole halfway down the vertical poles to stabilize the arch, and create a sturdy structure for these vigorous climbing plants.

5 Sow 2 or 3 beans directly into the compost at the base of each pole, after the last frost. If any fail to germinate, re-sow a few weeks later to give you a succession of beans.

6 Alternatively, start your beans off in pots indoors from mid-spring onwards, then harden them off and plant out after the last frosts. Tie the plants in to help them climb.

7 Water the plants in well and continue to water regularly, especially when the flowers start to appear. After 4–6 weeks, start feeding weekly with liquid tomato fertilizer.

8 Pick the young, succulent pods every 2–3 days to keep the beans coming. Later in the season, stop picking Borlotti pods and leave the beans to develop for drying.

9 If you have spare space in the containers, sow quick-growing crops, such as rocket, radishes, or mustard leaves at the base of your beans. Re-sow as they mature.

Don't just reuse and recycle....
Re-invent!

All plants need in **order to grow** is **compost**, **light**, and **water**, so as long as your **containers and planters** provide these, you can **use almost anything** to grow crops in. **Recycling old objects** is especially rewarding, as it allows you to be **truly creative**, and to grow your own **healthy produce** in a **sustainable** way. Here, **reclaimed oil drums**, stacked together, provide a good home for herbs, chillies, and tomatoes on a small plot.

Pallet planter

With a few adaptations, a wooden pallet makes an innovative planter, providing a living wall of crops that is right on trend.

Materials

Recycled wooden pallet
Landscape fabric
Multi-purpose compost

Scissors
Staple gun and staples
Small watering can

Plants

Strawberries
Tumbling tomatoes, lettuce
sage, thyme, and marjoram.

Pinks, violas, and
nasturtiums.
Seeds of your choice

1 Pallets are usually easy to come by. Try a reclamation yard or your local tip for a medium-sized pallet that is undamaged and has roomy slots for plants to colonize.

Sitting tight to a wall or fence on the patio, this vertical planter is a great way to grow strawberries, salads, tomatoes, and herbs to serve at a summer barbecue — whatever suits your palate!

2 The compost is contained in pockets attached to each rung of the pallet. Cut fabric pieces that measure a little more than the length of a section and twice the depth.

3 Use your first piece as a template to cut the rest of the pockets. Each piece is folded along its length to form a pocket, with the ends close against the sides of the pallet.

4 Position the first pocket in the top of the pallet. Ensure the fabric fits snugly at the ends with no gaps for compost to fall through.

5 Staple the pocket to one side using a staple gun; then turn the pallet over to fix the second side. Ensure the fabric is secure. It needs to be able to take the weight of the wet compost, as well as the plants.

SOAKING

Moisture is at a premium in confined growing spaces, so before you plant your crops, give them a good soaking. While they are still in their pots, stand them in a tub of water and leave them there until bubbles stop rising from the compost. Remove them and let them drain.

6 Work your way down the rungs, attaching a pocket to the sides of each section to create, in this case, 18 separate growing compartments. Stand the pallet upright.

7 Place the pallet in position and secure it safely to the fence or wall before starting to fill the pockets. Fill the top with compost, then use a small trowel and your hands to carefully fill the lower compartments.

8 Continue packing compost into the pockets to make use of every inch of space. Leave room at the top for watering.

9 Make a plan before you start planting to create an attractive balance of trailing plants, bushy herbs, and flowers. Put trailing plants higher up and shade-tolerant herbs lower down – seeds can be sown in the top.

10 Plant young lettuce plants by tucking them into the slots sideways and pushing the root ball down into the compost.

11 Make a bold statement with a diagonal line of variegated sage. Surround it with other herbs and trailing plants. Stand back and check the results as you plant.

13 Use a watering can with a long spout to soak each level of the pallet thoroughly, and pack extra compost into any spaces that appear after the soil has settled.

12 When you are happy with the way the side is planted, plant up the top with trailing plants, such as tumbling tomatoes, strawberries, and nasturtiums. You can also sow seeds of quick-growing crops, like salad leaves and radishes.

Care Advice

Tidy up To keep your pallet looking great, remove weak growth and straggly leaves, harvest crops regularly, and deadhead flowering plants

Harvesting Crop the lettuces by cutting individual leaves, leaving the plant to grow. Pinch the leaves from herbs as you need them, and harvest fruits regularly.

14 Keep watering! The slots at the front need particular attention to support a dense colony of plants in such a little space with no chance of rain reaching the compost.

Courgettes in a bag

Woven plastic shopping bags are strong and durable, and are large enough to grow hungry crops, such as courgettes. They are also easy to store in winter.

Materials

Woven plastic shopping bags
Multi-purpose compost
Liquid tomato fertilizer
Watering can

Plants and seeds

1 plant per bag (Grow them from seed, sown under cover in mid-spring, or buy them.)

Try 'Goldie' for golden fruits and decorative foliage or 'Defender' for an abundant crop of green fruits. Give your plants room to grow, planting them 90cm (3ft) apart.

2 Water the plant in and keep it well watered throughout the season, especially during hot spells, to prevent powdery mildew. Once the first flowers appear, feed weekly with liquid tomato fertilizer.

1 Fill the shopping bag with compost, leaving room at the top for watering. Plant out small plants, one per bag, when there is no longer a risk of frost, and firm them in.

Care Advice

Sow plants a few weeks apart to avoid gluts and to provide non-stop supplies of this versatile crop all summer long. Courgette flowers are edible too.

Courgettes will not thrive in cold, wet conditions, so make sure temperatures have really warmed up before you plant them out.

3 Snip off the fruit when it is young, thin-skinned, and tasty. Keep an eye on the plant as courgettes seem to grow into marrows as soon as you turn your back!

4 Harvest continually to encourage plants to produce more fruits. As each plant will produce up to 20 courgettes if fed and watered well, you may only need one.

Grow a sack of spuds

Large sacks are ideal for growing early potatoes. Fill a sack one-third full with compost, add three tubers, a deep layer of compost, two more tubers, then cover with a final deep layer of compost. Water the soil well.

Harvest after the plants have flowered and the top growth begins to fade. Dig out a few potatoes at a time with your hands, or cut the sack to release the entire crop.

Blueberry in a pot

Blueberries are ideal for large containers, where they flower and fruit freely, bearing delicious berries. They must have acid soil, which you can easily provide.

Materials

Large container
at least 45cm (18in) across
Ericaceous compost
Water butt to collect rainwater
Bamboo canes
Plastic netting

Plants

Blueberry plant
(You may need two)

Blueberries are acid-loving plants, and as well as needing lime-free ericaceous compost, they should also be watered using rainwater. Most tap water is alkaline.

1 Choose a container at least 45cm (18in) wide, ensuring it has drainage holes in the base. Make some if it doesn't. Add ericaceous compost to the bottom of the container.

2 To help avoid disturbing the roots of your plant, slide it from its pot. Place the pot in your container, sitting it on compost so its top sits 5cm (2in) below the container rim.

4 Turn the pot slightly to loosen it, then lift it out. You will be left with a pot-shaped hole, the ideal size, shape, and depth for your blueberry plant.

3 Fill around the blueberry's old pot with moist compost, firming it gently as you do so, until you have filled up to the top of it. This will ensure your plant is planted at the correct depth.

5 Lightly tease the rootball with your fingers to loosen the outermost roots, then place it in the container. Firm it in, then water the plant well.

Pollination

Blueberry flowers must be pollinated before they will set fruit. Some varieties are self-fertile, meaning you only need one plant. Most are not, so you will need to grow two.

Care Advice

Watering Keep plants moist at all times, watering them with rainwater.

Feeding Blueberries flower and fruit over a long period. As soon as the first blooms appear, start feeding them with a liquid tomato fertilizer each month.

Pruning Plants only need pruning after their second year. In spring, remove any weak, dead, and diseased growth. Prune fruited stems back to healthy buds, and thin out a third of the oldest stems.

6 Birds love blueberries and will take them as soon as they start to ripen. Protect plants using fine plastic netting or make a simple fruit cage.

DIY windowbox

Why buy when you can make? This simple rustic windowbox is easy enough for a DIY novice, and can be tailor-made to fit the space available.

Materials

Pre-treated wooden planks, 1.5cm (½in) thick
Tape measure
Pencil
Wood saw
Power drill with wood bits

Screws – 4cm (1½in) long
Screwdriver
Copper tape
Galvanized tacks
Sandpaper
Multi-purpose compost

Strong winds and visiting birds can dislodge a windowbox with disastrous results. If you're siting your box on an upper-storey sill, make sure that it is properly secured.

2 Lay the timber on a firm surface to support it while you cut the lengths you need. Hold the pieces together to ensure you have cut and measured them accurately.

3 Drill two pilot holes, about 6mm (¼in) in towards the ends of each long side of the box – these will help to prevent the wood splitting. Then screw the sides together to form a neat rectangle.

1 Make sure your windowsill is level, and able to support a box, before measuring it to decide on the length and depth of your windowbox. Two small boxes may be more practical than a long one. Measure and mark up the timber.

HANDY HERBS

Any cook would welcome a bed of mixed fragrant herbs growing just outside a window – much cheaper and fresher than shop-bought herb packs and pots.

4 Keeping the box square, screw the sides of the box together. If it wobbles or looks crooked, loosen the screws and re-adjust the joints. Then tighten all the screws.

5 When all four sides have been joined together, insert the base, and hold it in place firmly. First drill pilot holes, then screw through the sides, into the base, to secure it.

6 Screw small wooden batons across the base of the box to create feet. This allows water to drain easily and raises the base off the wet sill, helping to prevent wood decay.

7 Use a large drill bit to drill holes at regular intervals through the base of the box to provide good drainage to prevent plants becoming waterlogged.

9 Secure the tape by tapping in galvanized tacks, spaced evenly to create an attractive rustic finish. Sand the box lightly to remove splinters and smooth the edges.

8 To deter slugs and snails, stick a band of copper tape around the outside of the windowbox, keeping it level. A static charge from the copper repels the pests.

10 Fill the box almost to the top with compost, allowing space for watering, and plant it up with your chosen plants. Water well and place the box on the windowsill.

Squash trellis

Beautifully decorative and a great use of vertical space, training squashes up a trellis is a wonderful way to grow this vegetable in confined areas.

Materials

Large metal container
Bubble plastic
Multi-purpose compost
Wooden poles or canes
Soft string

Scissors
Liquid fertilizer
Mulch
Watering can

Plants

Squash plants
Nasturtiums (optional)

Squashes come in an exciting array of shapes and sizes, and can be easily grown from seed. Try acorn-shaped 'Mini Red Turban' or the trombone-like 'Tromboncino'.

2 Ensure each side of the metal container is insulated, then make small holes in the bubble plastic to allow water to drain freely. The container can then be placed in a sunny position and filled with multi-purpose compost.

1 Metal containers look attractive but can heat up quickly in hot weather. To keep the roots of your plants cool, insulate the container inside using bubble wrap plastic.

Growing Advice

Watering and feeding Water plants well, especially in hot dry spells, ensuring the compost never dries out. After 4–6 weeks, feed weekly with a liquid fertilizer to ensure a good harvest.

Training As the squash plants grow, tie their stems carefully to the trellis with string, covering it evenly.

4 Once the risk of frost has passed, plant your squashes, ensuring they are hardened off first. For smaller varieties, plant two plants per container, 30–45cm (12–18in) apart.

3 Insert tall wooden poles or bamboo canes upright into the container, then attach shorter laterals using string to create an open framework. Ensure it is sturdy and secure.

5 Water the plants in well and start training them vertically by tying their stems to the framework using soft string. Train them regularly to ensure they can support their fruits.

6 Mulch plants with compost to keep their roots cool and moist, and to provide extra nutrients.

Useful tips

Promote ripening
Snip off or move aside any leaves that cast shade on the fruits to help them ripen fully.

Bonus crop
In larger containers, plant nasturtiums alongside your squashes and enjoy their edible flowers.

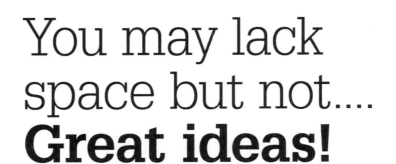

You may lack space but not....
Great ideas!

In order to **make the most** of a small plot, consider **every possible area** where you could **grow crops**, no matter **how unlikely**, then think **how to use it**. Most crops are **versatile** and **easy to grow**, especially annual ones, which means you can be **really inventive** in **how and where** you grow them. If, for example, you have a **garden table** that's only **used occasionally**, why not use part of it for a crop of **salad leaves**?

Growing gutters

Easy to fix to any sunny vertical surface, plastic guttering is ideal for growing super fast, feather-light crops such as microgreens and pea shoots.

Materials

Plastic guttering	Screws
Gutter ends	Screwdriver
Gutter brackets	Power drill
Pencil	Epoxy resin glue
Hacksaw	Multi-purpose compost
Drill	Watering can

Seeds

Peas
Microgreens – mustard greens, mizuna, rocket
Herbs – basil, fennel, coriander, parsley

Leaves picked in infancy have a flavour that is more intense than fully grown leaves. This is a great way to grow crops such as rocket that tend to bolt when they mature.

1 Measure your space and decide on the lengths and arrangement of your guttering. Mark the guttering with a pencil and cut the lengths using a hacksaw.

2 Hold the guttering firmly on a solid surface and use a power drill to make drainage holes in the base, spaced about 15cm (6in) apart along its length.

COURSING WITH BABY GREENS

Sited in sun or part-shade, gutters provide the ultimate economic growing space for the impatient gardener. Start harvesting microgreens and herbs within days, and resow the gutters up to three times for fresh or different crops. Then clear out the depleted compost, refill the gutters with fresh compost, and begin again.

Care Advice

Watering To keep your gutters cropping, water them gently but thoroughly every day.

Pests and diseases Microgreens grow fast and are harvested quickly, leaving little time for attack from pests and diseases. Slugs and snails will climb to the feast, so be vigilant and catch them *en route*.

3 White guttering is easy to paint to match your garden colour scheme. Use simple slot-on ends to keep the compost and water in, and glue them in place if need be.

4 Mark positions for the brackets, making sure the gutter is supported in the middle, and is level. Drill holes, screw in the brackets, and simply slot the gutters into place.

5 Fill the guttering with compost, leaving a small space below the rim for watering. Level it off and firm it gently. Your growing gutter is now ready for sowing seeds.

7 Check your plants within a few days to see if they have germinated. Thin out overcrowded seedlings, eating the thinnings, and leave the rest to grow on until ready to pick.

6 Sow seeds fairly densely – every shoot is part of the crop. (*Peas are shown here.*) Cover them lightly with compost, and water in using a can with a fine rose.

Corn salad leaves will keep cropping for weeks.

Sweet, delicate-tasting pea shoots are a gourmet crop.

8 Harvest within a week, depending on the crop. Pull microgreens out of the soil, including roots, and wash well before eating. Pick pea shoots and salad leaves when they are young and tender.

Productive paving

Herbs can bring your new paths and patios to life. Plant creeping and flowering herbs between the stone slabs for food and fragrance at your feet.

Materials

Paving slabs
Gravel
Landscape fabric
Trowel
Watering can

Plants

Creeping and flowering herbs, such as chamomile, Corsican mint, oregano, and variegated thyme.

Most herbs prefer a sunny spot, and are easy to care for. Plant a mix of flowering herbs, such as chamomile, and those with colourful foliage, such as variegated thyme.

1 Decide where your new patio or path will be, level the soil, and lay the landscape fabric. Cover the fabric with gravel and set your slabs into it, leaving small planting gaps.

2 Scoop out some gravel between slabs, cut slits in the fabric beneath, and dig small holes in the soil. Plant the herbs, and replace the fabric and gravel around their bases.

3 Water the herbs in well, and keep them moist until they show signs of new growth. Pinch out their growing tips to encourage new sideshoots, and trim back excess growth.

FRAGRANCE AT YOUR FEET

As well as providing you with tasty leaves and stems to add to your cooking, a herb-filled path makes a highly aromatic feature. Simply brushing over the herbs releases their fine fragrance into the air.

Hanging herbs

Many herbs prefer dry, hungry soil, and so thrive in hanging baskets. Position one near your kitchen window or door, and enjoy tasty herbs close to hand.

Materials

Hanging basket
Bracket
Multi-purpose compost
Trowel
Watering can

Plants

Golden oregano
Purple sage
Curry plant
Chives
Mint

Choose bushy and trailing herbs for an attractive effect, and pick silver-, gold-, and purple-leaved forms for visual impact. Hang the basket in a sheltered, sunny position.

2 Plant the herbs 5cm (2in) below the rim, with trailing types at the edges, bushier ones in the middle or at the back. Fill around them with more compost and firm them in.

1 If you don't already have one, fix a hanging basket bracket at your chosen location. Fill the base of the basket with multi-purpose compost, leaving space to plant the herbs.

3 Water the herbs well, leave it to drain, then add more compost between the plants if required. Attach the chains to the basket and hang it to give the best display.

KEEP YOUR HERBS HAPPY

Water plants regularly to encourage tender growth, but feed them just once a month with balanced liquid fertilizer. Pinch out the tips to promote bushiness, and pick the leaves and stems as you need them. Evergreen herbs, such as sage and rosemary, will give colour throughout the winter months.

Wall pockets

Wall-mounted planting pockets are now widely available, and are ideal for growing small crops on sunny vertical surfaces.

Materials

Wall pockets
Multi-purpose compost
Plastic ties and wire

Bamboo canes
(painted black - optional)
Water-retaining gel

Plants and seeds

Thyme plants
Rosemary plants
Sage plants
Viola plants

Chive plants
Strawberry plants
Microgreen seeds

Wall pockets are well suited to small annual crops and herbs, and there are many designs you can use. In autumn, they can easily be taken down and stored until the following spring.

1 Decide how much space you want to cover and buy enough planting pockets. Choose a design that suits the space and the plants you want to grow.

2 To save having to make lots of holes in your walls, the pockets are hung from a bamboo cane. Fix sturdy wires to hang the canes from.

3 Link the planting pockets together using strong plastic ties. If your pockets don't already have mounting holes, carefully make some, being sure they cannot easily rip.

4 Join as many pockets together as your cane and wire will safely hold – remember that wet compost is heavy. You could also mount them using a small stake and rope.

5 Attach the cane to the uppermost pockets using plastic ties. Fix a pair of level screws to the wall, then hang the pockets, using the mounting wires tied to the cane in step 2.

6 The pockets will quickly dry out once planted, so to help retain moisture, add some water-retaining gel crystals to the compost. Water the mix before using it to plant up.

Care Advice

Watering Keep the pockets well watered, checking them every day in warm spells. Water carefully early in the morning, using a can with a fine rose fitted.

Training Trim back plants that become tangled or look untidy. Deadhead and harvest the crops regularly.

7 Starting from the uppermost pockets, plant them up, leaving about a 5cm (2in) gap below the rim for watering.

8 Create a display of bushy and trailing plants, and crops grown for their leaves, flowers, and fruits. You can even include small specimens of shrubby herbs, such as sage.

CROPS IN
SMALL PLOTS

A nine-pot plot

If you don't have room for a conventional raised bed, you can create a similar amount of growing space by using large containers. Here, nine pots give the same space as a 1x1m (3x3ft) bed, and provide two abundant crops that last from spring to winter.

To **get the most** from your pots, **sow crops** to **harvest** in spring and summer, **doubling** the number of **vegetables** you can **grow** in **one year**. Use the **largest** containers you have **room for**, and **ensure** they have ample **drainage** holes.

You will need

- **Materials**
  Large containers
  Multi-purpose compost
  Bamboo canes
  Garden string

- **Tools**
  Trowel
  Scissors

CROPS – WHEN TO SOW OR PLANT

Radishes
Sow from mid-spring.

Lettuces
Sow from mid-spring.

Mangetout
Sow in early spring.

Spring onions
Sow from late spring.

Pea shoots
Sow batches in early spring.

Sugar snap peas
Sow in early spring.

Carrots
Sow from mid-spring.

Beetroots
Sow from mid-spring.

Kale
Sow from mid-spring.

French beans
Sow in early summer.

Runner beans
Sow in early summer.

Cavolo nero
Sow in spring in small pots.

Kai lan
Sow in early summer.

Cucumbers
Plant small plants in early summer.

Tomatoes
Plant out small plants in early summer.

African basil
Plant out in early summer.

Chillies
Plant small plants outside early summer.

French tarragon
Plant in early summer.

Spring pots

The more pea pods you pick, the more will be produced.

Add beetroot leaves and pea shoots to summer salads.

Just 4–5 lettuce plants will provide ample leaves.

Summer pots

Climbing crops, such as beans, are ideal for smaller spaces.

Leaf crops, such as kale, will thrive in cool containers.

Cut-and-come-again leaf crops make good use of limited space.

Alternative crops to grow

Spring

Rocket
Instead of spring onions This peppery-tasting leaf crop can be sown directly into their container during spring.

Mustard leaves
Instead of radishes Grow as a cut-and-come-again salad. Sow the seeds directly in the container, then thin the plants.

Swiss chard
Instead of kale Sow seeds directly into the container or plant small plants. This crop will last well into winter if left to grow on.

Summer squashes
Instead of peas or beans Train the plants up cane wigwams to make best use of small spaces. Water and feed the plants well.

Spinach
Instead of Kai lan Sow seeds into the container. Pick individual leaves or cut whole plants, allowing them to re-grow.

Kohl rabi
Instead of kale This unusual-looking vegetable is grown for its plump, tender stems. Sow seed in early summer.

Summer

Oriental greens
Instead of French tarragon This is a quick-growing leaf crop that can be re-sown repeatedly in summer, every 3–4 weeks.

Sweet basil
Instead of African basil If you cannot find the African form, this annual type can be sown directly in early summer.

Courgettes
Instead of peas or beans These are large plants that need plenty of watering and feeding. Plant in early summer.

Pot 1 Spring

Radishes are one of the quickest crops you can grow, and are ready to harvest in 4–6 weeks. Sow seeds directly in spring and harvest in early summer.

1 Radishes grow quickly, so thin them out as soon as seedlings are large enough to handle to prevent the plants competing.

2 Keep the plants well watered and pull the rotots once they reach a usable size. Pull some as baby roots, others once full size.

French beans can be started once the radishes are pulled. Add slow-release fertilizer to the compost and insert tall canes, tied into a wigwam, for support.

1 Seed can be sown in late spring under cover, ready to plant out. They can also be sown directly at the base of each cane, once the radishes are removed.

2 Position in a sheltered, sunny site, and water well. Feed weekly with liquid tomato fertilizer once the first flowers appear. Harvest the beans regularly to keep them coming until autumn.

Pot 2 Spring

Lettuces are quick and easy to grow. They can be harvested as baby leaves as soon as they are large enough, or as full-size heads after 9–12 weeks.

1 Sow the seeds thinly on the surface in spring. As the seedlings grow, thin them out, using the thinnings as a crop of baby leaves. Leave four plants to form heads.

2 Harvest the heads once large enough in early summer, or pick the outer leaves individually as and when you need them.

Pot 2 Summer

Runner beans crop well in pots if well watered. Young plants can be raised under cover in late spring to plant out, or sow the seeds directly in early summer.

1 Provide a tall support, tie in new growth, and keep the plants well watered. Once the first flowers appear, start feeding plants weekly with a liquid tomato fertilizer.

2 Harvest the pods regularly, once large enough to use. The more you pick, the more will grow.

Pot 3 Spring

Mangetout taste delicious, and although they are expensive to buy, they are very easy to grow. The seeds are sown directly in the container in spring.

1 All peas need something to cling onto when growing, so insert some twiggy sticks into the compost for support.

2 Keep plants well watered, especially once in flower. Pick the pods whole just as a peas inside begin to form.

Pot 3 Summer

Cavolo nero is a type of kale, grown for its rich-tasting leaves. It is slow-growing but can be picked as young or mature leaves from late summer until spring.

1 Sow seed in small pots in spring, thin out the seedlings to one per pot, and grow them on until the peas are harvested. They can then be planted into the container.

2 Water the plants well and provide taller plants with support. Harvest the outer leaves once large enough.

Pot 4 Spring

Spring onions are grown for their leaves and bulbs, which give a mild onion-flavoured crunch to salads. Red varieties give a welcome splash of colour.

1 Sow seed directly in the container during spring, and thin the seedlings to 2.5cm (1in) apart for the bulbs to reach a good size.

2 Keep the spring onions well watered, and pull the plants whole once the stems are pencil-thick. Loosen the compost if required.

CROPPING
If you pull the individual spring onions carefully when harvesting, any smaller plants can be left to grow on, making full use of the crop. Use thinnings like chives.

Pot 4 Summer

Kai lan, which is also known as Chinese broccoli, is grown for its succulent leaves, shoots, and flowers. Sown in spring, it is ready to crop in 8–10 weeks.

1 Sow seeds directly in the container and thin seedlings to 20cm (8in) apart. Keep them well watered, and check plants for caterpillars (*above*), which attack them.

2 When the stems reach 20–25cm (8–10in) tall, cut them back to 7.5cm (3in) high. Leave the plants to grow back, then harvest them again later.

Pot 5 Spring

Pea shoots are fantastically quick to grow, and are ready to harvest in about three weeks. The plants can be harvested two or three times during spring.

1 Soak the seeds overnight and sow them directly in the container, 2.5cm (1in) apart. You can use any pea seeds for pea shoots.

2 When shoots are 10–15cm (4–6in) tall, cut them just above the lowest leaves. Keep them well watered and they will regrow, giving 2–3 more crops.

WATER WELL

Pea shoots should be kept moist at all times to ensure they taste at their best. Regular watering also helps to prevent powdery mildew attacking the plants (*see p.245*).

Pot 5 Summer

Cucumbers need a warm, sheltered site, and a tall support to climb. Varieties with smaller fruits are the most productive, especially when harvested often.

1 Plant out small cucumber plants once the risk of frost has passed and the peas have been removed. Tie in their stems to the support at first.

2 Keep plants moist and feed weekly with liquid tomato fertilizer once the first flowers appear. Harvest the fruits when they reach a usable size.

Pot 6 Spring

Sugar snap peas produce sweet-tasting pods from late spring. They are easy to grow from seeds sown directly in the container in early spring.

1 Peas need support, so insert 3–4 twiggy stems into the container before sowing the seeds. Tie in the young stems, after which they will climb naturally. Keep the plants well watered.

2 Pick the pods when round and plump, but before the peas inside are firm. Harvest regularly to encourage cropping.

Pot 6 Summer

Tomatoes need a sheltered, warm site. Cordon varieties, grown as a single stem, are best for containers. There are many fascinating varieties to try.

1 Plant out a young plant in early summer, and insert a 2m (6ft) cane to support its single stem. Keep plants well watered and tie the stem to the cane as it grows.

2 Remove any sideshoots that form from the main stem. Feed plants weekly with tomato fertilizer after the first flowers appear. Harvest the fruits when they pull easily from the vine – pick often.

Pot 7 Spring

Carrots are sweet and tender when harvested young, and are ready to pull after 12 weeks. Early varieties tend to be short or round-rooted, so ideal for pots.

1 Sow seed thinly to avoid attracting carrot fly when you thin the plants (*see p.242*). The pest is attracted by the carrot scent.

2 Keep the plants well watered and pull the roots when they reach a usable size. Take care not to disturb any that are still growing.

SCENT TRAIL
To help prevent carrot flies from finding your crop, position it near strongly scented plants, such as African basil. Their scent will help mask the tell-tale carrot aroma.

Pot 7 Summer

African basil is a tender perennial with richly aromatic purple-tinted foliage. Like sweet basil, the leaves are great for salads, pestos, and sauces.

1 Only available as plants, plant one into your container in early summer once the risk of frost has passed. Place it in full sun, and water and feed it regularly.

2 Pinch out the tips to the encourage sideshoots, and pick the leaves and stems all summer. Bring the plant under cover for winter.

Pot 8 Spring

Beetroots can be ready to pull in as little as eight weeks, when the roots are sweet and tender. The leaves can also be lightly picked, and used like Swiss chard.

1 Sow seeds directly in the container and thin the seedlings to 5–10cm (2–4in) apart. You can add the thinnings to salads.

2 Keep the plants well watered to ensure the roots are tender, and harvest them as soon as they are large enough to use.

MICRO BEETS

Although beetroots are usually grown for their plump roots, you can also grow them as a micro crop. Pull after 2–3 weeks and eat the leaves, stems, and tiny roots.

Pot 8 Summer

Chillies come in a dazzling selection of shapes, sizes, and colours. When growing outdoors, give them a warm and sheltered position to crop at their best.

1 Chillies need a long growing season, so start seeds off indoors in early spring, or buy small plants. Plant out hardened-off plants after the last frost in early summer.

2 Water the plants regularly, and feed them weekly with liquid tomato fertilizer once the first flowers appear. The fruits can be harvested when green and milder in taste, or when fully ripe and hot.

Pot 9 Spring

Kale is usually grown as a winter crop (*see p.141*), but if sown in early spring, the outer leaves can also be harvested repeatedly until early summer.

1 Sow seeds under cover in pots during late winter, harden off the seedlings, and plant them into the container in early spring.

2 Once the plants are large enough, start cropping the older outer leaves, leaving the young inner ones to grow on.

Pot 9 Summer

French tarragon is a delicious half-hardy herb that benefits from being grown in a container. Use the leaves in chicken and fish dishes, or in soups and salads.

1 Best bought as young plants in early summer, plant them into the container once the risk of frost has passed. Pinch out the tops of the stems for bushier plants.

2 Keep the plants moist and feed regularly with a balanced liquid fertilizer. The leaves and stems can be picked as needed. Bring the plant indoors in winter.

Crops sown early spring will give a bountiful harvest at the end of the season. Many can be picked over several weeks.

The outer leaves of lettuces can be picked individually.

Try yellow-rooted beetroots as well as classic red forms.

Peas and mangetout crop for weeks when picked regularly.

Yield Summer

Most summer crops can be harvested over many weeks, rewarding your efforts with ample fresh and tasty produce.

Try different basils, such as lemon, lime, purple, and Thai.

Kale can be picked as soon as the plants are large enough.

Tomatoes give a delicious, summer-long harvest.

Where space allows use....
Raised beds

There are **many advantages** to growing your crops in a **raised bed** (*see pp.20–23*), but as well as providing ideal **growing conditions**, they can also make a **handsome feature**. When choosing what to grow, consider varieties with **attractive qualities**, such as **colourful foliage** or **flowers**, and **combine crops** with different leaf **textures**. Rather than **planting in rows**, why not arrange your crops in **interesting patterns** instead?

DIY raised bed

Sunny walls provide warmth and shelter, encouraging plants to grow. It's the ideal place to position a three-sided raised bed, which you can easily make yourself.

You will need

- **Materials**
Pre-treated timber planks at least 5cm (2in) thick.
Long wood screws
Wooden batons
Plastic sheeting

Topsoil, compost, and grit
Rubble (optional)

- **Tools**
Power drill, saw, tape measure, and a shovel

Raised beds can be made from many different materials. Timber is ideal, as it is easy to use, and when treated with preservative, it can be very long-lasting.

1 The bed consists of a three-sided wooden frame placed against a wall to form a box. Decide how large you want your bed to be, then measure, mark up, and saw the pieces of timber to length on a firm, level surface.

2 Depending on how high you want your bed to be, join the first three sides at the corners to form a frame. Drill pilot holes, then fix the sides using long screws. Repeat this if you are making a deeper bed using two or more frames.

3 Choose a level site and place the first frame in position against the wall. Place your second, and even third, frame on top. Make certain that each added frame sits squarely on the one below it.

4 With all the frames in place and squared up, cut wooden batons, two per side, to join them together. Drill pilot holes first, then firmly screw the batons in place.

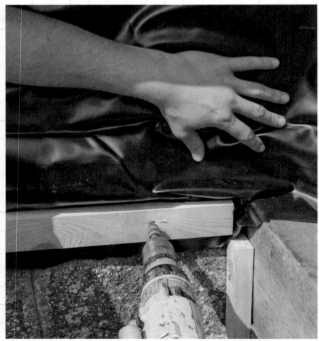

5 Cut plastic sheeting and a piece of baton the full length of the bed. Screw the baton to the wall, through the lower edge of the plastic sheeting, to hold it in place.

6 Fold the first piece of plastic sheeting down and into the bed, so that it covers the wall. This will prevent the wall becoming damp. Now cut more plastic sheeting to fully line the inside of the bed and nail it in place. This will protect the wood from decay and help to retain moisture.

OPTIONAL EXTRA

To take full advantage of the warmth and shelter provided by a sunny wall, consider installing some trellis before positioning the bed. This will allow you to grow climbing crops, including heat-loving melons, perhaps. Alternatively, rather than trellis, you could also attach horizontal wires to the wall. Wires are more flexible than trellis, and are ideal for training fruiting crops, such as raspberries and Japanese wineberries.

8 Fill the bed with a mixture of topsoil, compost, and grit (*see p.23*), mixing it in a wheelbarrow first. Water the mix, allow to settle for a few days, then top it up if required.

Care Advice

Timber care Even pre-treated timber benefits from being painted with wood preservative each year. This is best done in autumn, when the bed is likely to be empty. Use a wood preservative harmless to plants.

7 If the bed is more than 90cm (36in) deep, place some rubble in the bottom to ensure good drainage.

The easy-to-grow bed

Planted with crops that are quick and easy to grow, this bed will supply you with an abundance of nourishing and tasty leaves and fruits from spring to winter.

When **planting** your bed, be aware that **strawberry plants** are perennial, and take up **permanent space**. Use the space around them for **quick-growing** crops. **Sow** new batches of **seeds** as soon as **space is available**, and always sow a **few extras** in case of **slug** and **snail** damage. **Surplus** plants can be **thinned**.

Spring

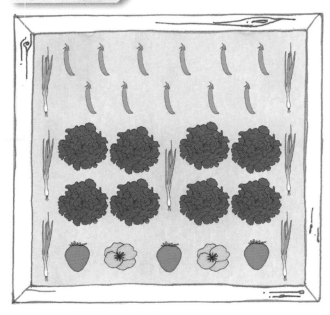

GETTING STARTED Plant the strawberries, which will remain in the bed all year. Sow the seeds of your spring crops directly in the soil, ready to harvest a few weeks later.

You will need

- **Materials**
  Raised bed, approximately 1m (3ft) square
  Compost, soil, and grit
  Bamboo canes
  Fine plastic netting

- **Tools**
  Spade
  Trowel
  Watering can
  String guides

Summer

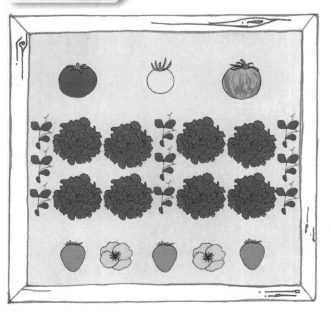

GETTING AHEAD Remove the spring crops, plant out the tomato plants, and sow your summer crops. Sow Swiss chard and mustard leaves in pots to plant out in autumn.

Autumn

EXTENDING THE SEASON Leave the strawberries where they are but remove all other summer crops. Plant out the Swiss chard and mustard leaves sown in pots in summer.

CROPS – WHEN TO SOW OR PLANT

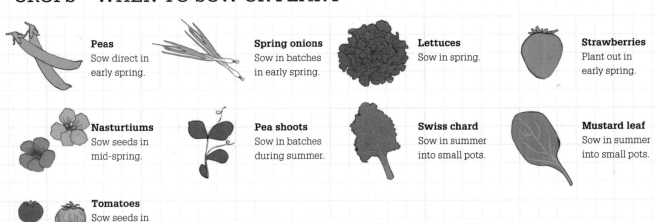

Peas
Sow direct in early spring.

Spring onions
Sow in batches in early spring.

Lettuces
Sow in spring.

Strawberries
Plant out in early spring.

Nasturtiums
Sow seeds in mid-spring.

Pea shoots
Sow in batches during summer.

Swiss chard
Sow in summer into small pots.

Mustard leaf
Sow in summer into small pots.

Tomatoes
Sow seeds in mid-spring.

Use string to help work out your plant spacings.

Remove any weeds that appear before sowing and planting.

Fill your bed with the ideal soil to get the best results, (see p.23).

Spring

Now is the time to start sowing the first seeds and planting strawberries. To give your crops a useful head start, warm the soil first (*see pp.44–45*).

1 Strawberry plants need time to establish, so plant them first. You can then sow your annual crops in the remainder of the bed around them.

2 Once the soil is warm enough, sow your seeds into shallow drills, to the depth and spacing recommended on the packet. Water them in gently.

SOW UNDER COVER

If the weather is cold, start your seeds off under cover, ready to plant out in a few weeks. Peas can even be started in old guttering.

Use plastic netting to protect crops from birds and animals.

Use bamboo canes to mark out where to sow your seeds.

Plant strawberries 30–40cm (12–14in) apart and water in.

3 Snip off strawberry "runners", the long stems with young plants attached, so the plants put all their energy into producing berries.

4 Thin out your vegetable seedlings as they grow, leaving the strongest ones at the recommended planting distances (*see pp.32–34*).

5 Don't waste the "thinnings", the surplus seedlings removed during thinning. Many, such as lettuces, can be harvested as baby vegetables.

Spring

Sugar snap peas can be harvested and eaten whole, as soon as the juvenile peas start to swell within the pods. Wait until the pods have plumped up slightly, and eat them on the day they are picked for the best flavour.

GROWING SPRING ONIONS

Weed around spring onions, being careful of their shallow roots, so that they don't have competition for nutrients and water. Sow batches every few weeks from spring to summer for a constant supply. If you have enough space, you could also continue sowing throughout summer.

GENERAL CARE

DON'T FORGET TO:

- Keep all plants well watered
- Weed between plants carefully
- Regularly check for signs of pests
- Pick fruiting crops regularly
- Deadhead flowering plants
- Re-sow new batches of seed
- Ensure nets are securely fastened

SPRING LETTUCES Crop lettuces by picking the outer leaves, rather than pulling up the whole plant, and leave the inner ones to continue growing. Alternatively, cut the head off near the base, leaving the stump to re-sprout.

Sow nasturtium seeds between your strawberry plants.

Picking the outer leaves creates space for other crops.

Summer

Once the peas have been harvested, remove the plants and replace them with young tomatoes. Continue to harvest the outer lettuce leaves.

1 Harvest the spring onions by pulling them from the soil. Prepare the area for re-sowing by removing any plant debris, and lightly forking the soil.

2 Sow a new batch of spring onions, or another quick-growing crop, such as pea shoots. These too can soon be replaced, once harvested.

3 Water your tomato plants regularly, especially in drier weather. Erratic watering when their fruits start to form can cause them to split and spoil.

Sow Swiss chard in pots. Use them to replace the lettuces.

Train the tomatoes as space-saving cordons (*see p.171*).

Deadhead your nasturtiums to keep them flowering well.

4 Harvest pea shoots just above the lowest leaves, when they are about 15cm (6in) tall. The plants will re-sprout to give another harvest in a few weeks.

Edible nasturtium flowers, oakleaf lettuce, and pea shoots make a colourful salad.

Always wash your hands after handling tomato plants. The sap can irritate skin. Or, wear gloves.

Swiss chard can be harvested as baby leaves to eat raw, or fully grown to enjoy lightly steamed.

Tomato tips

Choice toms
Try growing unusual varieties of tomatoes, such as 'Green Zebra' (*above*), that you'd be hard pressed to find in the shops.

Ripe fruits
Small cherry tomatoes are the best type for cooler areas, as they ripen more quickly than larger-fruiting forms.

TRAIN TOMATOES

When there isn't a lot of room for bush varieties, cordon tomatoes are an excellent option. These are grown as a single stem that is trained up a vertical support, such as a cane or string. Any sideshoots that appear in the leaf joints should be pinched out (*left*), and the main growing tip is removed once the plant has produced 5–6 trusses of tomatoes. If you have more space, bush tomatoes simply require support rather than training.

Autumn As summer crops finish, plant out hardy ones raised from seed in pots during summer, such as Swiss chard, to harvest until winter.

The Swiss chard will benefit from winter protection.

Mustard leaves will continue to grow during mild spells.

The strawberry plants will become dormant until spring.

The soil in your raised bed will still be warm in autumn, and although the temperatures are lower, it is still warm enough to grow certain crops. Take advantage of these favourable conditions for as long as they last, and grow and harvest as much as you can.

Alternative crops to grow

Spring

Carrots
Instead of peas Sow seeds thinly where they are to grow in spring. Pull in early summer.

Beetroots
Instead of peas Sow seeds into the soil in early spring. Pull the tender roots in early summer.

Radishes
Instead of spring onions Sow the seeds directly, water well, and pull when large enough.

Violas
Instead of nasturtiums Plant out young plants in early spring. Pick the flowers into summer.

Summer

Marjoram
Instead of pea shoots Plant out plants in early summer. Pick the aromatic leaves all summer.

Spinach
Instead of lettuces Sow into the bed in mid-spring and harvest from summer to autumn.

Sweet basil
Instead of nasturtiums Plant young plants in summer and harvest regularly all season.

Sweetcorn
Instead of tomatoes Plant out young plants in early summer in a block. Harvest in late summer.

Autumn

Winter-flowering violas
Instead of mustard leaves Plant in autumn and harvest the flowers until spring.

Cavolo nero
Instead of Swiss chard Sow seed in pots in early summer to plant out in late summer.

Rocket
Instead of mustard leaves Sow the seed into any free space and harvest once large enough.

DECIDING WHAT TO PLANT

No sowing plans are set in stone and it's important to grow what you love to eat. If you're not interested in growing spring onions, lettuces, tomatoes, or peas, here are some alternatives to try.

Gourmet bed

When space is limited, think gourmet, and fill your bed with crop varieties that you could never find in the supermarket. They offer a superior taste and often look fantastic, but take no more time and effort to grow than ordinary crops.

Look out for **unusual** or **heirloom** varieties of **tomatoes**, **carrots**, and **beetroots** to enjoy their **subtly different tastes**, **colours**, and **textures**. Why grow the same **courgettes** that you can **easily buy**? Try **tromboncino** ones instead, with their **amazing fruits**, and grow them **alongside** lemony-tasting **purple oxalis** leaves.

Squash flowers are a foodie's delight. Pick male flowers on long stems for stuffing, leaving the female flowers to form fruit.

You will need

▪ **Materials**

Raised bed, approximately 1m (3ft) square
Multi-purpose compost, topsoil, and grit
Liquid fertilizer

3 x bamboo canes, about 8ft (2.5m) tall
Garden string
Trellis
Cloche for spring protection

Spring to summer

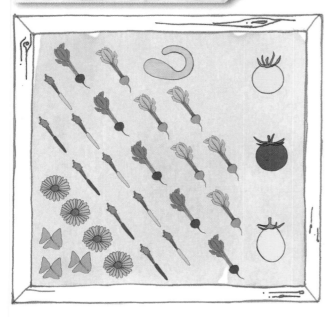

Autumn to spring

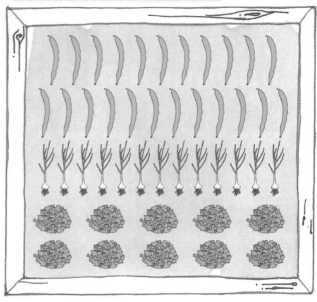

READY FOR SUMMER After the last frost, plant the tomato and tromboncino courgettes, and provide support. Also plant the oxalis. The other summer crops can be sown from seed.

INTO WINTER Keep your bed productive with frilly endives, sown in autumn for winter harvest, and garlic and broad beans, which will be ready next spring and summer.

CROPS – WHEN TO SOW OR PLANT

Courgette 'Tromboncino'
Sow mid-spring.

Tomato 'Black Cherry'
Sow mid-spring.

Beetroot 'Boltardy'
Sow mid-spring.

Endive 'Wallone Despa'
Sow/plant late summer.

Tomato 'Snowberry'
Sow mid-spring.

Pot Marigolds
Sow early spring, plant late spring.

Beetroot 'Burpees Golden'
Sow mid-spring.

Broad bean 'Super Aquadulche'
Sow in late autumn.

Tomato 'Beam's Yellow Pear'
Sow mid-spring.

Carrot 'Harlequin'
Mid-spring.

Purple oxalis
(Oxalis triangularis)
Plant late spring.

Garlic
Plant in late autumn.

Reclaimed steel mesh is ideal for courgettes to climb.

Fill with an even mix of compost and topsoil, and 10% grit.

Spring

Tomatoes and courgettes can be grown from seed in spring, or bought as young plants. After the last frost, harden them off and plant them out.

1 Tomatoes and summer squashes are hungry plants, so add home-made compost or enriched multi-purpose compost to the bed.

2 Make a hole for the courgette wider and deeper than the pot. This vigorous plant will fill the space, so don't be tempted to plant two.

3 Plant with the neck of the plant just above the surface of the soil to avoid neck rot. Firm it in well and water it thoroughly using a can.

Grow marigolds from seed indoors or buy plants in spring.

Plant all your small plants into the bed before sowing seeds.

Sink tall bamboo canes into the bed to support tomatoes.

4 Plant your tomatoes next to their canes and tie in the stems with string. Water them well and continue to tie them in as they grow.

5 Harden off your marigolds and oxalis plants, and plant them out after the last frost. Snip off any dead leaves to encourage new growth.

6 Sow carrot and beetroot seeds in drills, cover them lightly, and water gently. Check planting distances in the Crop planner (*see pp.224–241*).

By early summer your bed will be bursting with produce, rewarding your hard work. Harvest regularly, and keep your crops well watered and fed.

Summer

1 Your squash will cling on and climb rapidly, but watch out for growth heading off in a direction you hadn't planned on; redirect it and tie it in.

2 Thin out carrots and beetroots to allow decent-sized roots to form. Eat tiny carrots raw and add young beetroot leaves to salads.

3 Start feeding tomatoes weekly with a tomato fertilizer once the first flowers appear. Keep the plants moist at all times to stop the fruits splitting.

5 Lightly harvest the leaves from oxalis to use sparingly in summer salads. The leaves pack a strong, lemony punch, which comes from oxalic acid (also present in sorrel and spinach). Enjoy eating it in moderation.

WHY RED?

Tomatoes come in a huge variety of colours and shapes – from dark red to pale yellows and greens, and in all shapes from plums to light bulbs. All are grown in the same way, so why not choose one that isn't simply round and red?

4 Tromboncinos are at their best when they are 30–40cm (12–16in) long. Keep picking for a non-stop supply. Try shaving them with a potato peeler to use like pasta.

WEEDING OUT WEEDS

A benefit of planting closely in your bed is that it helps to suppress weeds. However, they can still appear, unseen at first, between your plants, and will compete for water and nutrients. Check regularly, and remove any you spot.

6 The mix of soil in a raised bed, and its lack of stones, makes it ideal for growing carrots with perfectly formed roots. For a selection of colourful, crunchy, and sweet-tasting roots, grow 'Harlequin' (*right*). If you would prefer single colours, choose 'Cosmic Purple', 'Atomic Red', or 'Solar Yellow'.

Colourful gourmet crops will turn a simple bed into a garden spectacle.

Summer

From mid- to late summer there should be something to eat every day: fresh beetroots and carrots, and trusses of tomatoes ripening in the sun.

1 Pull beetroots when the tops of the roots are visible above the soil surface. You can also eat the leaves young and raw or mature and cooked.

2 Pull carrots gently to avoid snapping the roots and disturbing the rest of the crop. Make this easier by watering the soil or loosening it slightly first.

3 To encourage a larger harvest, pick your tomatoes regularly. To enjoy them at their best, pick when they are fully ripe, pull easily, and slightly soft.

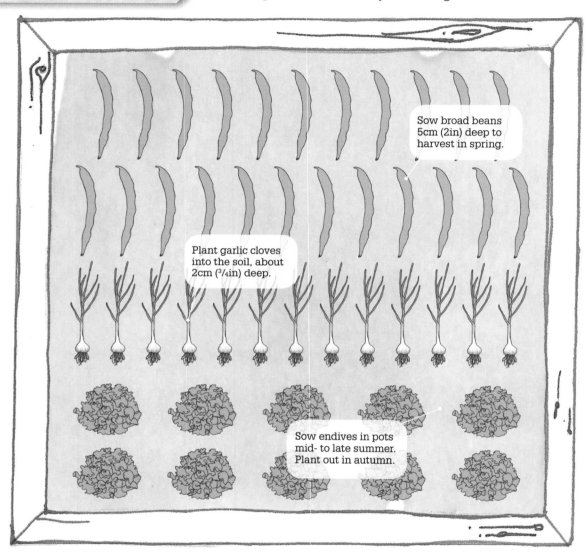

Clear the bed in autumn and dig in fresh compost for crops that will take you through to next summer.

Sow broad beans 5cm (2in) deep to harvest in spring.

Plant garlic cloves into the soil, about 2cm (¾in) deep.

Sow endives in pots mid- to late summer. Plant out in autumn.

Sow broad beans from mid-autumn to crop in early spring. A late-autumn planting of garlic will be ready to harvest in summer, while endive will keep you in flavoursome leaves throughout the winter. In colder spells, protect your plants with fleece or cloches.

Alternative crops to grow

Spring to Summer

Cornflowers
Instead of marigolds Use these attractive edible flowers to add colour to salads. Sow in spring.

Sweet peppers
Instead of tomatoes Peppers enjoy the same conditions as tomatoes. Plant in early summer.

Kohl rabi
Instead of carrots Sow this gourmet vegetable directly from mid-spring onwards.

Spinach
Instead of endive Sow seed in pots during summer and plant seedlings out in early autumn.

French or runner beans
Instead of tromboncinos Use either crop to cover the vertical support. Sow in early summer.

Alpine strawberries
Instead of oxalis These can be planted as young plants during spring, and will fruit all summer.

Summer herbs
Instead of oxalis Plant thyme and marjoram in spring, and harvest throughout summer.

Florence fennel
Instead of carrots Sow directly in early summer, keep moist, and harvest the stems in summer.

Winter to Spring

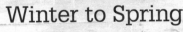

Chicory
Instead of endive Sow in pots in summer, ready to plant them out when the bed is cleared.

Cavolo nero
Instead of broad beans Sow in pots in summer. Insert canes for support and harvest all winter.

Swiss chard
Instead of endive Sow during late summer in pots, and plant them out in early autumn.

Sprouting broccoli
Instead of broad beans Raise plants in pots from seed sown in summer. Harvest until spring.

Circular salad bed

A raised bed can be used to create dazzling decorative effects that are also productive. Try growing your own crop circles – rings of mixed salad leaves and edible flowers, with tumbling tomatoes on the perimeter. Site the bed in a sunny spot on a patio, so you can nip out and pick leaves as and when you need them.

In plots where **space** is **limited** there is **always** a **compromise** between **how much room** you devote to **flowers**, and how much you **allocate to crops**. The **virtue** of this **planting scheme**, with its **colourful** and **edible fruits**, **leaves**, and **flowers**, is that it **tastes** as **good as it looks**.

Try planting tomato 'Terenzo', a sweet hanging variety that is perfect for tumbling over the edge of a raised bed.

You will need

▪ Materials

Raised bed, approximately 1m (3ft) square
Multi-purpose compost, topsoil, and grit
Horticultural sand

Liquid fertilizer
Cloches and fleece for winter protection

Spring to Summer

Autumn to Winter

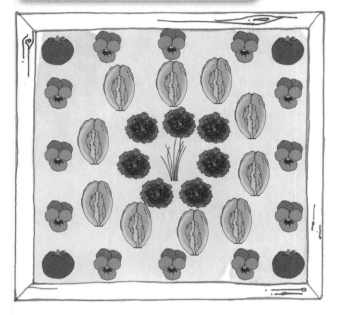

FRESH SALADS are the main focus of the summer bed, sown and planted from mid- to late spring to provide a continuous supply of leaves and sweet cherry tomatoes.

COLOURFUL KALE and spicy mustard leaves, sown in summer and planted in autumn, maintain a handsome bed and bear salad crops and stir-fry vegetables through winter.

CROPS – WHEN TO SOW OR PLANT

 Tomato 'Terenzo' Plant late spring.

 Lettuce 'Lobjoits' Sow mid-spring.

 Lettuce 'Navarra' Sow mid-spring.

 Violas Plant out in mid-spring.

 Chives Plant out in mid-spring.

 Garlic 'Solent White' Plant in autumn.

 Kale 'Redbor' and 'Winterbor' Sow midsummer.

 Mustard leaves 'Red frills' Sow in summer.

 Mibuna Sow in summer.

The sand planting guides will wash away after sowing.

Tomatoes can be grown from seed or bought as plants.

Summer

For summer crops, work begins in late spring, preparing your bed for sowing seeds directly into the soil, and for planting out plants after the last frosts.

1 If using an existing bed, prepare the soil by digging it over, remove any weeds, and top it up. For a new bed fill it with the ideal mix (*see p.23*).

2 Rake the soil to a fine crumb, ready for sowing. Attach string to a peg in the middle of the bed and tie a dibber to the other end. Mark out circles.

3 Check your seed packets for the ideal planting distances for your crops. Space the circles accordingly, and mark them out using sand.

Violas flower early and can be picked from late spring.

Cut chives regularly and use the flowers in summer salads.

Leave sideshoots on tomatoes for bushy, tumbling plants.

4 Put a chive plant in the centre of the bed, with a tumbling tomato plant in each corner to cascade over the edges. Firm and water the plants in.

5 Sow lettuce seeds thinly into the drills, following the lines of the sand. Cover with soil and water in gently using a can fitted with a fine rose.

GENERAL CARE
DON'T FORGET TO:
- Keep to the circles as you sow, and remove seedlings that spoil the design
- Protect young plants from slugs, snails, and pigeons
- Keep watering, even in wet spells
- Weed between plants regularly
- Harvest young salad leaves regularly
- Give tomatoes a liquid feed when the first flowers and trusses begin to form

8 Keep deadheading violas for a continuous supply of edible blooms. If the heads turn to seed, the plant will stop flowering.

6 Space the viola plants evenly around the edge of the bed in a wide circle. Tuck them into holes, firm them in, and water them thoroughly.

9 Cut the chives as and when you need them. For a fresh new crop, cut the leaves right down in midsummer – they will quickly grow back. Chives will overwinter, and can be divided up in spring and replanted in fresh compost in a sunny position.

7 As lettuces begin to grow, thin them out so that the remaining plants can mature fully. Use the thinnings as an early crop, adding the succulent, sweet leaves to salads.

LETTUCE GROW ON
Rather than pulling up the whole head of your lettuce plants in one go, you can leave the plant in place and harvest the outer leaves as you need them. Alternatively, cut the head off near the base, leaving a short stump that will re-grow. Good varieties to plant include speckle-leaved 'Freckles' and bronze-tipped 'Rubens Red'.

Winter

As crops begin to fade at the end of the summer, clear the bed of debris and top it up with compost, ready to plant crops for winter and next summer.

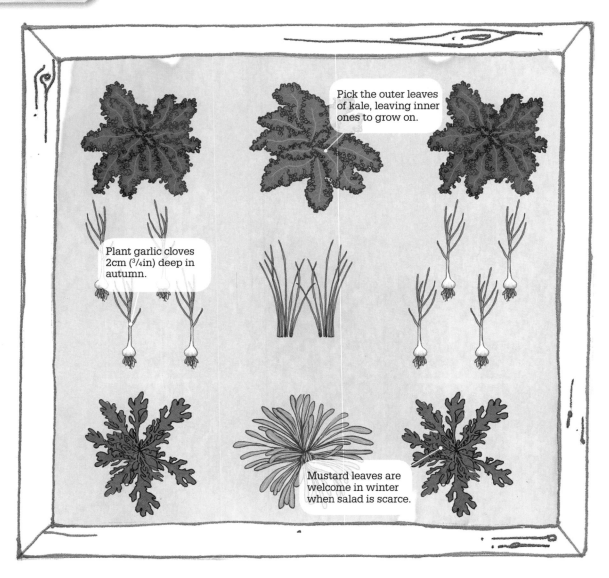

Pick the outer leaves of kale, leaving inner ones to grow on.

Plant garlic cloves 2cm (³/₄in) deep in autumn.

Mustard leaves are welcome in winter when salad is scarce.

For crops to grow through winter, sow kale and mustard greens in small pots during summer and grow them on, ready to plant out once your summer crops have been cleared. Garlic can be planted directly in autumn. Protect your salad leaves with fleece or cloches during winter.

Alternative crops to grow

Summer

African basil
Instead of chives Plant out a pot-grown specimen once the risk of frost has passed. Harvest the leaves and stems during summer.

Coriander
Instead of chives Sow seeds directly in early summer and keep the plants moist. Enjoy the flavoursome leaves all summer.

Strawberries
Instead of tomatoes Plant strawberries in spring, and choose summer- and perpetual-fruiting varieties for the longest harvest.

Spinach
Instead of summer lettuces Sow the seeds directly in late spring and keep the plants well watered. Harvest summer to winter.

Hyssop
Instead of violas Plant out small plants during spring and harvest the richly aromatic leaves and flowers throughout summer.

Winter

Swiss chard
Instead of kale Sow the seeds into small pots in summer, grow them on, and plant out in autumn. Harvest the leaves in winter.

Sprouting broccoli
Instead of kale Sow the seeds in pots in summer and grow them on. Plant in autumn, staking them, and harvest winter and spring.

Endive
Instead of mustard leaves Sow the seeds during summer into small pots outside. Plant them out once the bed has been cleared.

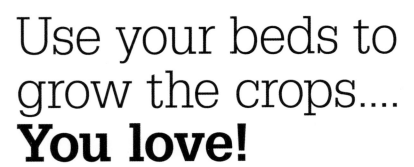

Use your beds to grow the crops....
You love!

One of the **pleasures** of **growing your own** is that you can **concentrate** on **the crops** that you really **enjoy eating**. Lettuces may be **easy to grow**, but if you don't like them, **why bother**? Growing your own also means you can experiment with **different varieties** that you **never see** in the shops. If you love summer salads, **explore every possibility**, from textural Asian greens, to peppery mustard leaves. **If you like it, grow it**.

The Med bed

This bed brims with an essence of the Mediterranean, with its vibrant colours and flavours. Best in a warm spot, site your raised bed in the sunniest and most protected corner. Hold back from planting and sowing until the sun is high and the soil has warmed up in late spring.

Chillies come in a dazzling array of colours and sizes but select carefully. They can pack a real punch that ranges from mild to super hot!

Tap into the **tastes** and **health benefits** of a **Mediterranean diet**, by growing **vibrant chillies** and sweet **peppers**, crunchy **Florence fennel**, and **glossy aubergines**. Look for varieties that have been **selected** to **grow outdoors** in slightly cooler climes, and **pamper your plants** during prolonged **wet and cooler** spells.

You will need

- **Materials**
Raised bed approximately
1m (3ft) square
Topsoil, compost, and grit
Watering can
Liquid ferilizer

Bamboo canes
Soft string
Fleece or cloches for
protection

Summer

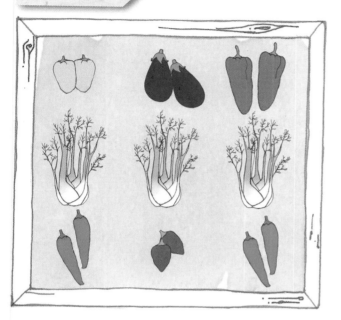

Winter

START THE SUMMER BED in late spring with chillies, bought as small plants, and Florence fennel, sweet peppers, and aubergines grown from seed indoors and planted out.

FOR WINTER CROPS clear the bed in early autumn and sow radicchio and winter lettuce. Plant out kale, chicory, and sprouting broccoli, grown in pots during summer.

CROPS – WHEN TO SOW OR PLANT

Sweet Pepper
Sow indoors in pots early spring.

Florence fennel
Sow indoors in pots early spring.

Chicory
Sow in pots in midsummer.

Lettuce
'Merveille de Quatre Saisons'
Sow seed directly in autumn.

Chilli Pepper
Plant out plants in late spring.

Sweet Pepper
Sow indoors in pots early spring.

Kale
Sow in pots in midsummer.

Sprouting broccoli
Sow in pots in midsummer.

Chilli Pepper
Plant out in late spring.

Aubergine
Sow indoors in pots early spring.

Radicchio
'Orchidea Rossa'
Sow in autumn.

DON'T DISTURB

Aubergines dislike root disturbance. Plant seeds singly in pots indoors in spring, and ensure the plants have a good root system before you plant them outside. Acclimatize the plants to life outdoors by hardening them off over a couple of weeks. Plant out gently in warm soil in full sun, and insert a cane for support.

English summer This bed is definitely one for warmer areas – in cooler spots or during a cold, wet summer you may struggle to produce a ripe aubergine or more than a handful of sweet peppers. It's worth having a go, and if any plants flag or fail, replace them with Mediterranean herbs, such as rosemary and basil, and sow fast-growing salad leaves.

TOO CHILLY FOR CHILLIES?

Both chillies and sweet peppers are tender plants and suffer in cold, wet soil. Harden them off well before planting, and make sure that the soil in your bed has warmed up. Putting a cloche over the planting area for a week or two will help to create a welcoming spot.

Summer

In early summer, Florence fennel can be sown from seed under cover, to plant out in a few weeks' time. Later harvests can be sown directly.

1 Sow three fennel seeds per pot under cover in late spring and thin to one healthy seedling, or sow directly outdoors in early summer.

2 Plant out with minimal disturbance after the last frosts. Fennel plants tend to bolt if they are disturbed, or are too cold or underwatered.

SOME LIKE IT HOT AND DRY

Chillies hate to be wet, so water this crop minimally and let the top of the soil dry out between waterings. Most chillies ripen from green to red, becoming spicier as they do so. As long as the fruits have reached their full size, you can pick them when they are green for a milder flavour. Picking unripe fruits will also encourage the plant to keep flowering and produce more chillies.

When your aubergine is about 25cm (10in) tall, pinch out the top of the main shoot to encourage bushier growth. Once the plant starts flowering, feed it weekly with liquid tomato fertilizer to promote fruiting.

FUSS OVER FENNEL

Fennel likes to be pampered, so keep your plants well watered, and mulch around the base of bulb to retain moisture. Pick some leaves to use in salads or to flavour food, leaving plenty to support the plants' growth. Harvest, by pulling the bulbs out of the soil with the roots attached, or cut through the base of each bulb just below ground level. The remaining roots should then produce another small flush of airy aniseed-flavoured leaves.

Some sweet peppers grow tall and may need supporting with a bamboo cane. Feed plants regularly with tomato fertilizer once in flower, and harvest the mature fruits to encourage more.

Winter

As soon as the last peppers have been picked, fill the bed with kales, broccoli, chicory, and lettuces for a feast from autumn to spring.

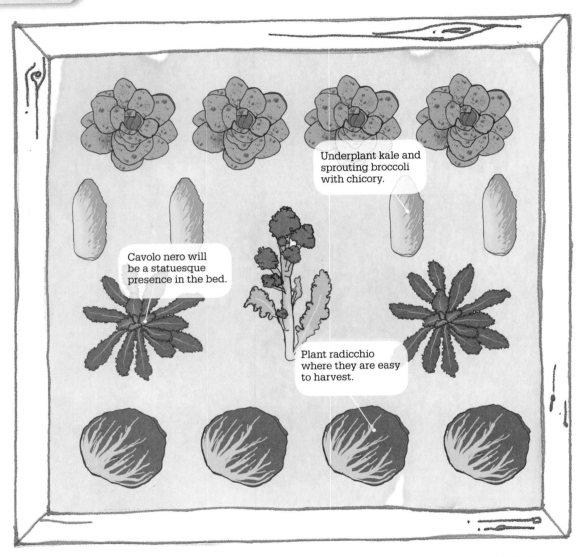

Underplant kale and sprouting broccoli with chicory.

Cavolo nero will be a statuesque presence in the bed.

Plant radicchio where they are easy to harvest.

In early autumn clear the bed and dig in fresh compost. With planning, your winter crops will be underway, sown and growing in pots from midsummer. In autumn, some winter salads can be sown directly. Protect plants with fleece or cloches in cold spells.

Alternative crops to grow

Summer

Runner beans
Instead of peppers Sow beans directly in late spring and train the plants up wigwams.

Tomatoes
Instead of aubergines Plant cordon tomatoes in late spring. Tie them in to bamboo canes.

Summer squashes
Instead of peppers Train the plants up trellises or wigwams to make the best use of space.

Sweetcorn
Instead of aubergines Sow seeds in early summer or plant out small plants raised in pots.

Cucamelons
Instead of fennel These delicate vines will scramble up a wigwam or trellis. Sow in spring.

Sweet basil
Instead of chillies Sow indoors, plant out mid-spring, and pinch out tops for bushy growth.

Dwarf French beans
Instead of chillies No supports needed for these productive plants about 45cm (18in) high.

PLANTING OPTIONS
If aubergines and fennel are not to your taste, there's a range of crops shown here that will thrive in similar warm, sunny conditions through summer, or which will fill the bed in winter. See the Crop planner on pages 224–241 for more alternatives to grow.

Winter

Swiss chard
Instead of kale Start off Swiss chard in small pots in summer for colourful stems and tasty leaves.

Corn salad
Instead of radicchio Sow seed during summer in modules and transplant in early autumn.

Mustard leaves
Instead of lettuces Interplant broccoli with spicy green and red varieties. Sow in summer.

Red Russian kale
Instead of broccoli Sow red and purple kales in pots in summer for a vibrant winter bed.

Shady bed

Not every gardener can rely on full sun throughout the day, especially on urban plots surrounded by houses and fences. This bed embraces shadier spots, with plantings of vegetables, such as lettuces, sorrel, and mustard leaves, that thrive in cooler growing conditions.

Try for a **decorative effect** in your **cool corner** by planting quadrants of **shade-tolerant** crops that are **gloriously tasty** too. Red-flecked **Lettuce 'Speckles'** and red-leaved **'Navarra'** are **stars** of the summer bed. **In autumn Mizuna** 'Red Knight', **Mustard leaf** 'Green in Snow', and **pak choi** continue the show.

Fancy salad leaves are a feast for the eyes in shady spots. Try 'Freckles', a lettuce with dainty speckled leaves.

You will need

- **Materials**

A raised bed approximately 1m (3ft) square
Topsoil, compost, and grit
Garden string
Short bamboo canes

Watering can
Fleece and cloches for winter protection

Spring

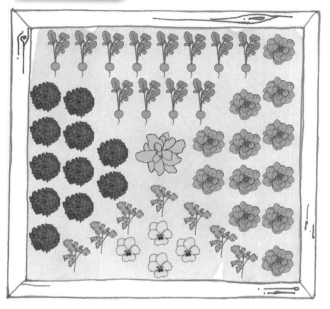

GETTING STARTED After the last frosts, plant small parsley plants, violas, and a sorrel centrepiece. Sow radishes and lettuce varieties to harvest in early summer.

Summer

REPLENISH While the soil is still warm in late summer, clear the bed and resow it with autumn and winter crops, such as mustard leaves, pak choi, and mizuna.

CROPS – WHEN TO SOW OR PLANT

Sorrel
Plant small plants
or sow seeds in
mid-spring.

Violas
Plant small plants
or sow seeds in
mid-spring.

Parsley
Plant or sow
in mid-spring.

Radishes
Sow at intervals
from spring to
late summer.

Lettuces
Sow regularly
from spring until
midsummer.

Pak choi
Sow seeds direct
in late summer.

Mizuna
Sow mid- to late
summer.

Mustard leaves
Sow seeds
direct in late
summer.

Sow parsley seeds or plant out small plants in spring.

Mark out areas by running string from corner to corner.

Sorrel is a perennial herb that bears tangy, lemony leaves year after year.

Spring

Mark out your plot and plant potted herbs before sowing seeds. Your seedlings should start appearing within a week, and radishes may be ready in 3-4 weeks.

1 Sow seeds in clearly defined rows. This makes it easy to identify weeds and pick them out so that there is no competition for nutrients and water.

2 When the seedlings are bigger and have developed true leaves, thin them out carefully, leaving the remainder at their final spacings.

3 Radishes put on rapid growth. As soon as seedlings appear, thin them out to 5cm (2in) apart to allow space for roots to develop quickly.

Sow more radishes every two weeks for a non-stop harvest.

Thin out the lettuces to their preferred planting distance.

Keep cutting the tops of parsley to stop it going to seed.

4 Don't throw away your thinnings. These young tender leaves, along with young radish and sorrel leaves, make a delicious herby salad.

5 Brighten up your salads with sweet-scented viola flowers in all shades from violet to pale yellow. Pick them regularly to keep the plants flowering.

6 Harvest radishes young, as soon as their crowns show above the soil. Left to grow too big, the roots become tough and will lose their crispness.

HARVEST LETTUCE by picking off the outer leaves and leaving the heads to grow, or by cutting the fully-grown hearty head off at the base. If you leave the stump in the soil it will regrow, giving leaves to harvest repeatedly in summer.

Spring

Keep up a non-stop supply of salad crops by resowing whenever space becomes free.

1 Radishes take little room and grow fast in the summer heat, so after each harvest, level and rake over the soil and sow a fresh row.

2 Resow lettuces too, keeping them well-watered to prevent them bolting and going to seed.

Shady areas are havens for slugs and snails. Go on patrol after rain or at dusk and deal with them.

Summer

As soon as the last lettuces and radishes have been harvested, seize the opportunity to sow more leafy vegetables that will take you through autumn.

1 Dig some fresh compost into the bed and rake it to a fine tilth before sowing sugarloaf chicory, mustard leaves, and pak choi.

2 When the seedlings have developed their first true leaves thin them to 15–30cm (6–12in) apart. Use the thinned seedlings for salads.

3 Pak choi leaves will be ready in about a month; fully-grown heads for stir-frying take up to two months. Water well to prevent bolting.

Alternative crops to grow

Summer

Sweet Cicely
Instead of Sorrel Plant this delicious aniseed-flavoured herb as a small plant in spring.

Tatsoi
Instead of lettuce Directly sow this gorgeous oriental, known as rosette pak choi, in early spring.

Spinach
Instead of lettuces Sow spinach from spring onwards. Use young leaves in salads.

Oriental saladini
Instead of lettuces Grow a mix of mustard leaves and oriental greens to cut-and-come-again.

Lettuce 'Maravilla de Verano Canasta'
Instead of 'Freckles' Try this red- and green-leaved variety.

Swiss Chard
Instead of lettuces Sow in spring to supply young leaves and brilliantly-coloured stems.

Chervil
Instead of parsley This ferny herb has an aniseed flavour. Sow in spring and summer.

COOL CUSTOMERS

For your shady bed seek out varieties that have been selected for their resilience in cooler climes, especially for your autumn crops. A cool corner in summer can become a frost pocket in winter. Use fleece and cloches to protect delicate leaves.

Autumn

Corn salad
Instead of chicory Sow seeds directly in late summer for crops throughout the winter.

Rocket
Instead of mustard leaves Sow seed directly from mid- to late summer and pick regularly.

Winter purslane
Instead of chicory Eat both the leaves and flowers of this crop, sown directly in summer.

Kales
Instead of pak choi Grow one of the many varieties of kale, sown directly in midsummer.

Liven up your cooking with....
Fresh herbs!

Instead of growing **fruit and vegetables**, you could devote a raised bed to **culinary herbs**. Choose your favourite **annual and perennial** types, such as **basil** and **chives**, and also include **evergreens**, like sage, that you can **pick during winter**. Many **common herbs** can be **bought fresh** in supermarkets, so why not plant others that aren't, such as **aromatic sweet Cicely**.

Tasty herb bed

This decorative, deliciously scented and intensely flavoured group of plants is tailor-made for a small bed. Keep them close at hand for easy picking. This a valuable crop for any cook who likes to experiment – cut herbs in shops are pricey, limited in scope, and bear no comparison to home-grown.

Many of these herbs are **perennials**, returning **year after year**, which makes this bed **easy to maintain**. Plant staples, like **sage and thyme**, and unusual herbs, such as **lovage**, **fennel**, **and sweet Cicely**, which you are **unlikely** to ever find **in the shops**. **Edible flowers**, such as borage, **self-seed freely**, giving **plants for free** the next year.

Spikes of fragrant thyme and vivid borage flowers are magnets for bees, attracting pollinators to all your crops.

You will need

• Materials
Raised bed approximately 1m (3ft) square
Topsoil, compost and grit.
Stakes for tall plants

• Tools
Watering can
Trowel

Summer

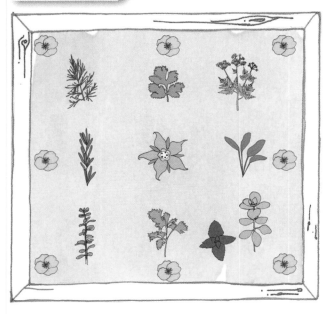

Winter

PLANTING UP Plant small herb plants in mid-spring as the soil warms up. Wait until after the last frosts to plant basil and fennel. Sow California poppies around the herbs.

WINTER HERBS Replace borage, coriander, and poppies when they go to seed with sowings of mustard leaves and rocket. Leave the perennials, and plant garlic in late autumn.

HERBS – WHEN TO SOW AND PLANT

Rosemary
Perennial, plant mid-spring.

Lovage
Tall perennial, plant mid-spring.

Sweet Cicely
Perennial, plant mid-spring.

Marjoram
Perennial, plant mid-spring.

Mustard leaves
Annual, sow in late summer.

Bronze fennel
Perennial, plant mid-spring.

Borage
Annual, sow late spring.

Purple sage
Evergreen shrub, plant mid-spring.

California poppy
Annual, sow in late spring.

Rocket
Annual, sow in late summer.

Thyme
Perennial, plant mid-spring.

Coriander
Annual, sow or plant late spring.

Purple basil
Annual, plant late spring.

Garlic
Plant cloves in autumn.

Give tall plants such as fennel plenty of growing room.

Plant out tender herbs like basil after the last frosts.

Indispensable to cooks, spicy rosemary can be grown from cuttings taken in summer.

Summer

Source a mix of small hardy and annual herb plants from a good herb nursery to plant in mid-spring, spaced evenly around the bed.

1 Mediterranean plants such as thyme, rosemary, sage, and fennel need full sun to grow to their best. Ease them gently from their pots.

2 This group of herbs is sensitive to wet soil, and should not be planted any deeper than they were in their original containers.

3 To help pot-grown plants establish well, use your fingers to gently loosen their rootballs. This encourages new roots to grow into the soil.

Celery-flavoured lovage grows tall so plant it at the back.

Thyme varieties include orange, lemon, and caraway.

Try tricolour, tangerine, and blackcurrant sages.

4 Purple basil is slower-growing than the green-leaved form. Make sure it isn't smothered by neighbouring plants as they grow.

5 Leave fennel to develop beautiful flowerheads in late summer. These are loved by bees, and will supply aniseed-flavoured seeds for cooking.

GENERAL CARE
DON'T FORGET TO:
- Keep all your plants well watered
- Check for slugs and snails regularly
- Keep trimming your herbs to prevent them flowering early
- Remove dead or fading leaves
- Pick herb bunches in late summer and dry for winter, or freeze them
- Cover tender shoots, like basil, with a net if pigeons start feasting on them

1 Keep on top of weeding to remove any competition in the bed for nutrients and water.

2 Young borage leaves bring a mild cucumber flavour to salads, and the flowers can be picked off and frozen into ice cubes to decorate fruity drinks. If you have too much borage, dig young plants back into the soil as a green manure.

MAKE THE MOST OF MARJORAM

Marjoram 'Golden Curly' is a decorative, perennial herb. It produces prolific tufts of bright leaves and frothy pale pink flowers that hum with bees in summer. Marjoram is in the same family as oregano and adds rich flavour to pasta sauces, pizzas, casseroles, and roasted vegetables.

Sowing annual herbs

Starting Sow seed under cover during early summer into trays of multi-purpose compost. Keep the seeds warm and moist.

Grow on Transplant the seedlings into individual pots once they are large enough to handle. Keep them under cover.

Bushy Pinch out the tips to encourage the plants to bush out. Harden them off for a few days, then plant them outside.

Winter

Fennel, hyssop, and sweet Cicely die down in autumn and shoot again in spring, while rosemary and sage can be picked all winter.

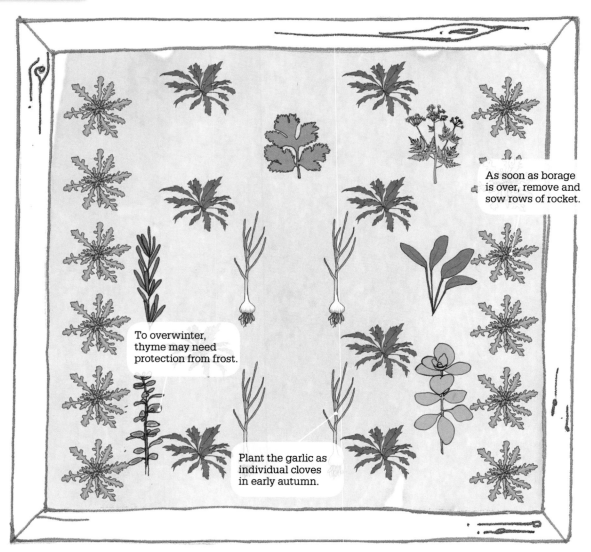

As soon as borage is over, remove and sow rows of rocket.

To overwinter, thyme may need protection from frost.

Plant the garlic as individual cloves in early autumn.

At the end of summer, gaps left in the bed by annuals can be sown with mustard leaf and rocket seeds for autumn pickings. In late autumn, plant garlic cloves, which can be cropped as green leafy spikes in spring, and as succulent bulbs in summer.

Alternative herbs to grow

Summer

Violas
Instead of California poppies Plant violas in spring and crystallize the flowers for cakes.

Tree spinach
Instead of lovage This fast-growing, 1.8m (6ft) annual has magenta-coloured young leaves.

Dill
Instead of fennel Sow in spring for aniseed-flavoured, feathery leaves and seeds.

Mint
Instead of sweet Cicely Keep mint confined to its pot in the bed to prevent it taking over.

Angelica
Instead of lovage This whooper produces sweet stems to cook with fruit and vegetables.

Salad burnet
Instead of marjoram Sow this pretty perennial herb with a mild cucumber flavour in mid-spring.

Hyssop
Instead of rosemary Plant in early summer. It has aromatic leaves and blue flower spikes.

Parsley
Instead of coriander Sow this versatile biennial in late spring. Use in sauces and salads.

Winter

Swiss chard
Instead of rocket Harvest the robust stems and crisp leaves in winter. Sow in late summer.

Kale
Instead of mustard leaf Kales have wonderful textures and colours. Sow in late summer.

Tatsoi
Instead of garlic Plant mid- to late summer for succulent leaves in autumn and winter.

PICK YOUR FAVOURITES
Choose your own. There are so many delicious herbs, each with their own flavour and special culinary uses, but the most useful to you are the ones you include regularly in your own dishes. Most are easy to grow and many come back year after year.

PLANT
KNOW-HOW

Crop planner

Use this crop planner to help make the most of the space you have, and to decide what to sow and plant when. With careful planning, you'll be able to make use of every inch of your growing space, with new crops ready to plant out as existing ones are reaching maturity.

A guide to the icons

 PLANT IN SUN OR PART SHADE All plants prefer either sun or part shade. Fruit and vegetables will not grow in full shade.

 TIME FROM SOWING TO HARVESTING This is a guide to how long each crop takes to reach maturity. Use it to plan the order in which you sow your crops.

 WHEN TO SOW SEED UNDER COVER This is when to sow seed in trays and pots. Keep the seedlings indoors until planted out.

 WHEN TO SOW SEED OUTSIDE Now is the time when you can sow each crop directly outside in the soil.

 WHEN TO PLANT OUT SEEDLINGS If you have raised plants from seed, or bought them as seedlings, this is when to plant them out.

 WHEN TO HARVEST This is the time of year when each crop should be ready to harvest.

 IDEAL DISTANCE BETWEEN PLANTS This is the distance to leave between your plants.

 SMALL-SPACE RATING This is a guide to how productive a crop is, relative to the time and space they need. The crops awarded three stars are the most productive choices.

SWEET PEPPERS

- ☼ Full sun
- ⧖ 20–26 weeks
- ⌂ Late winter to mid-spring
- ⚘ Late spring to early summer
- ⚲ Early to midsummer
- ⚱ Midsummer to early autumn
- ↔ 35–45cm (14–18in)
- ★★ Small-space rating

Varieties to try
'Corno di Toro Rosso' Long, tapering, scarlet peppers.
'Gourmet' Early-ripening, chunky, orange fruits.
'Gypsy' Heavy-cropping, slim green peppers ripen to red.
How to grow Once planted out support plants with canes, as the fruits are heavy, and feed weekly with tomato fertilizer once the first flowers appear. You get more peppers if you pick them green, but fewer, sweeter fruits if you let them ripen and change colour.

CHILLI PEPPERS

- ☼ Full sun
- ⧖ 20–26 weeks
- ⌂ Late winter to mid-spring
- ⚘ Late spring to early summer
- ⚲ Late spring to early summer
- ⚱ Midsummer to early autumn
- ↔ 35–45cm (14–18in)
- ★★★ Small-space rating

Varieties to try
'Apache' Dwarf habit and small red fruits (medium-hot).
'Hungarian Hot Wax' Ripening to red and good for cool areas (mild).
'Prairie Fire' Masses of tiny yellow to red fruits all summer (hot).
How to grow Treat in a similar way to sweet peppers (above). Dwarf varieties also thrive on sunny windowsills in pots as small as 15cm (6in) across. Harvest over several weeks, green and mild, or hot and ripe. The fruits become fewer but hotter if kept on the dry side.

TOMATOES

☀ Full sun
⏳ 9–12 weeks
🏠 Early spring
🌱 Mid- to late spring
🌿 Midsummer to autumn
🍅 Midsummer to early autumn
↔ 30–90cm (12–36in)
★★★ Small-space rating

Varieties to try
'Sungold' Sweet-tasting orange cherry-sized fruits.
'Gardener's Delight' Very reliable red cherry tomatoes.
'Green Zebra' Bears colourful yellow and green fruits.
How to grow Plant out deeper than in original pots, just below the first leaves. To grow cordon types, provide a tall support, and pinch out any sideshoots that develop, leaving a single stem. Once it has produced 5–6 trusses of fruit, pinch out the main tip. When growing bush varieties, the sideshoots are allowed to grow, and each will need a support. Keep all plants very well watered to prevent the fruits from splitting and, once in flower, feed weekly with tomato fertilizer.

AUBERGINES

☀ Full sun
⏳ 24–28 weeks
🏠 Early spring to mid-spring
🌱 Late spring to early summer
🌿 Late spring
🍆 Late summer to mid-autumn
↔ 60–75cm (24–30in)
★ Small-space rating

Varieties to try
'Bonica' An early variety with purple-black fruits.
'Moneymaker' Tasty, purple fruits; grows well outdoors.
'Thai Green Pea' Abundant, slender, lime-green fruits.
How to grow Plants need rich, well-drained soil, warmth, and humidity, so are usually grown under cover in cooler areas, or outside in sheltered, sunny spots. They dislike root disturbance, so sow seed singly in pots, planting them into containers or growing bags when the first flowers appear. Outdoor plants must be hardened off. Provide support and pinch out the growing tips to encourage bushiness. Water and feed well, and nip off the main tip once each plant has 4–6 fruits.

COURGETTES

☀ Full sun
⏳ 8–12 weeks
🏠 Late spring
🌱 Early summer
🌿 Early summer
🥒 Midsummer to mid-autumn
↔ 90cm (36in)
★★ Small-space rating

Varieties to try
'Goldy' Prolific crops of bright yellow courgettes.
'Zucchini' Green fruit and an early cropper.
'Tondo di Toscana' Pale green round fruits, good for stuffing.
How to grow Harden off young plants before planting out in late spring, after the last frosts, protecting them against slugs and snails. These are big plants, so position 90cm (3ft) apart, although they can also be grown in large containers. Keep plants very well watered, watering them directly at the base, and feed them regularly with a liquid tomato fertilizer once in fruit. Harvest courgettes when they reach 13–15cm (5–6in) long, taking care not to damage the main stem.

SUMMER SQUASHES

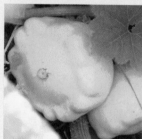

☀ Full sun
⏳ 14–20 weeks
🏠 Mid-spring to late spring
🌱 Late spring to early summer
🌿 Early summer
🎃 Midsummer to mid-autumn
↔ 90cm (36in)
★★ Small-space rating

Varieties to try
'Eight ball' Round, deep green, glossy squashes with nutty flesh.
'Peter Pan' Creamy-fleshed pale green, round, early squashes.
'Sunburst' Yellow patty pan-type squashes with white flesh.
How to grow These fast-growing, large plants can be planted in the soil, or in containers or growing bags. Sow the large seed into pots, planting them out once the danger of frost has passed, or sow them directly outside. These plants are hungry and thirsty, but prone to rot, so keep the leaves and stems dry when watering the soil. Apply mulch and feed weekly with tomato fertilizer. Train the stems vertically to save space and to keep the fruits off the soil, where they may rot.

CUCUMBERS

- ☀ Full sun
- ⏳ 16–20 weeks
- 🌱 Early spring to mid-spring
- 🏺 Late spring to early summer
- 🌾 Early summer
- 🍂 Midsummer to mid-autumn
- ↔ 45cm (18in)
- ★★★ Small-space rating

Varieties to try
'Burpees Tasty Green' This bears long, tasty crisp fruits.
'Crystal Apple' Outdoor type with small, round, sweet-tasting fruits.
'Marketmore' Outdoor ridge type with classic long, crisp fruits.
How to grow Cucumbers come in greenhouse or outdoor varieties; outdoor ones include short, rough-skinned ridge types. All need warmth, ample watering, rich soil, and a long season, so are sown indoors. Train the stems up canes to save space, and pinch out the tips when they reach the top. Keep plants well watered and feed regularly with tomato fertilizer. When growing greenhouse types, remove the male flowers (no fruitlet on stalk) to avoid bitter fruits.

CUCAMELONS

- ☀ Full sun
- ⏳ 12–16 weeks
- 🌱 Mid- to late spring
- 🏺 n/a
- 🌾 Late spring to early summer
- 🍂 Midsummer to early autumn
- ↔ 30–40cm (12–16in)
- ★ Small-space rating

Varieties to try
None available – Only the species is grown.
How to grow Although exotic-sounding, cucamelons are easy to grow, and can be treated in the same way as you would an outdoor cucumber. Sow indoors in late spring and plant out after the last frosts into borders or large containers. The fruits are produced on long, thin, delicate vines that can be trained up tall supports, through other climbers, or allowed to trail. Keep plants well watered, and feed them using liquid tomato fertilizer to encourage a larger harvest. The green fruits, which have a sharp cucumber flavour, are ready to harvest when they reach the size of a hen's egg, and can be added to salads.

PEA SHOOTS

- ☀ Full sun or light shade
- ⏳ 1–2 weeks
- 🌱 All year
- 🏺 All year
- 🌾 Not applicable
- 🍂 All year
- ↔ 2cm (1in)
- ★★★ Small-space rating

Varieties to try
'Oregon Sugar Pod' A hardy, disease-resistant mangetout type.
'Cascadia' A compact sugar snap pea that does not require support.
'Sugar Bon' A sugar snap pea, usually grown for its pods.
How to grow Sow any variety in succession every few weeks for a supply of tender shoots, leaves, and tendrils. Indoors, sow anytime in containers or growing bags, 4cm (1½ in) deep, and 5–8cm (2–3in) apart. Sow outdoors in containers or open ground from early spring to early autumn, or hardy varieties in mid- to late autumn for early spring shoots. Keep seedlings moist and harvest when 10–15cm (4–6in) tall, pinching off the top 5–8cm (2–3in). You can re-harvest 3–4 times.

PEAS

- ☀ Full sun or part shade
- ⏳ 12–14 weeks
- 🌱 Spring or mid- to late autumn
- 🏺 Spring
- 🌾 Mid-spring or late autumn
- 🍂 Early summer to mid-autumn
- ↔ 5cm (2in)
- ★★ Small-space rating

Varieties to try
'Kelvedon Wonder' Dwarf early or maincrop variety with small peas.
'Snow Wind' Mangetout variety, almost leafless, with sweet pods.
'Sugar Ann' A sugar snap pea with pale, succulent pods.
How to grow Sow seed under cover, 4cm (1½ in) deep, into cardboard tubes or biodegradable pots to avoid disturbing their roots when planting out. Seed can also be sown directly outdoors in single or double rows, 5–8cm (2–3in) apart. Support taller varieties with canes, trellis, or netting, and mulch young plants to retain moisture. Keep plants well watered once in flower and as the pods swell, and crop regularly to encourage a prolonged harvest.

FRENCH BEANS

- ☀ Full sun or part shade
- ⏳ 10–16 weeks
- ⌂ Mid-spring to midsummer
- 🌱 Late spring to early summer
- 🌿 Late spring to midsummer
- 🍂 Midsummer to autumn
- ↔ 5–10cm (2–4in)
- ★★★ Small-space rating

Varieties to try
'Cosse de Violette' Beautiful purple bean with pink flowers.
'Cobra' Stringless green beans with mauve flowers.
'Roquencourt' Dwarf variety with yellow pods.
How to grow Sow seed undercover, two per 10cm (4in) pot, harden them off, and plant outside after the risk of frost has passed. Climbing varieties will require support. Seed can also be sown outside after the last frost. Sow 2–3 seeds at the base of each support, and protect them against slugs. Tie in the stems as they grow, then pinch out their tips when they reach the top of their support. Harvest the beans regularly, while they are young and tender, to encourage a larger harvest.

RUNNER BEANS

- ☀ Full sun or part shade
- ⏳ 10–16 weeks
- ⌂ Mid-spring to midsummer
- 🌱 Late spring to early summer
- 🌿 Late spring to midsummer
- 🍂 Midsummer to autumn
- ↔ 15cm (6in)
- ★★★ Small-space rating

Varieties to try
'St George' Good cropper with red and white flowers.
'Polestar' Stringless and tasty variety with bright red flowers.
'Sunset' Reliable cropper with attractive apricot flowers.
How to grow Vigorous but also tender, so sow under cover, two seeds per 10cm (4in) pot. Harden the seedlings off and plant out after the risk of frost has passed, when seed can also be sown directly outside. Provide a tall support of canes or netting, and tie in new growth until plants start to climb themselves. Earlier flowers may not be pollinated if the weather is too cold for bees, and will fail to fruit. Sow batches 3–4 weeks apart for beans throughout the whole summer.

BROAD BEANS

- ☀ Full sun
- ⏳ 12–28 weeks
- ⌂ Late winter to mid-spring
- 🌱 Early spring to late spring
- 🌿 Late winter to mid-spring
- 🍂 Late spring to late summer
- ↔ 25cm (10in)
- ★ Small-space rating

Varieties to try
'Jubilee Hysor' Flavoursome variety with large pods and fat beans.
'Stereo' This has thin-skinned pods that can be eaten whole.
'The Sutton' Dwarf variety with nutty, white beans.
How to grow Broad beans have long roots, so sow them singly in long tubes under cover, or in deep beds of rich, free-draining soil outside. Early crops can be sown in autumn, but since they will not stand waterlogging or cold winters, protect those sown outdoors with cloches or fleece. Water well during flowering for a bigger crop. When the first beans appear, pinch out the tops to encourage the pods to grow, and to deter blackfly. Pick regularly while the pods are tender.

RADISHES

- ☀ Full sun or part shade
- ⏳ 2–8 weeks (summer); 8–10 weeks (winter)
- ⌂ Midwinter to early spring
- 🌱 Mid-spring
- 🌿 Mid- to late spring
- 🍂 Late spring to midwinter
- ↔ 1cm (½in) summer; 23cm (9in) winter
- ★★★ Small-space rating

Varieties to try
'Mino Early' Winter radish with long, white, tapering roots.
'Pink Beauty' Summer type with sweet, pink-skinned roots.
'Scarlet Globe' Bright red summer radish with round roots.
How to grow Summer radishes grow rapidly, producing small roots to eat raw in salads. The roots soon become tough, so sow batches every 2–3 weeks, even using them to fill gaps between larger crops. Early crops can be sown indoors, ready to plant out once the risk of frost has passed. Later sowings can be made outside. Winter radishes are large and slow growing, and are eaten cooked. Sow them thinly outdoors from mid- to late summer, thinning them to 23cm (9in) apart.

CARROTS

- ☀ Full sun or part shade
- ⏳ 12–20 weeks
- 🌡 Not applicable
- 🌱 Mid-spring to late spring
- 🌿 n/a
- 🖐 Late spring to early winter
- ↔ 5–10cm (2–4in)
- ★★ Small-space rating

Varieties to try
'Bangor' Maincrop carrot with smooth skins that store well.
'Sugarsnax 54' Bright orange, long roots with very sweet flavour.
'Parmex' Round, sweet baby carrots that crop early.
How to grow Choose round-rooted varieties for containers, and those with long roots for beds, which can also be harvested early as "baby" roots. Sow seed thinly, where they are to grow, in containers and beds, and them keep moist to encourage germination. For spring crops, sow autumn to winter; sow throughout spring and summer for later harvests. Protect early crops from frost using fleece, and install a barrier of fine netting to deter carrot fly larvae that attack the roots.

BEETROOTS

- ☀ Full sun or part shade
- ⏳ 8–12 weeks
- 🌡 Early spring
- 🌱 Mid-spring to summer
- 🌿 Mid-spring to midsummer
- 🖐 Midsummer to autumn
- ↔ 5–10cm (2–4in)
- ★★★ Small-space rating

Varieties to try
'Chioggia' Round-rooted with stripy pink and white flesh.
'Boltardy' This reliable variety is resistant to bolting.
'Burpees Golden' This variety has distinctive yellow roots.
How to grow Seeds can be sown directly outdoors from mid-spring, and also in modules to plant into any available space. Sow every few weeks and harvest the roots throughout summer and autumn. Each seed actually contains up to five individual seeds, so thin out the seedlings to leave one strong plant, spaced 10cm (4in) apart. Plants spaced more closely can be harvested as baby roots; further apart for larger, mature roots. The foliage is edible and can be lightly picked.

POTATOES

- ☀ Full sun
- ⏳ 12–22 weeks
- 🌡 n/a
- 🌱 n/a
- 🌿 Spring
- 🖐 Early summer to mid-autumn
- ↔ 30–40cm (12–16in)
- ★ Small-space rating

Varieties to try
'Charlotte' A salad potato with waxy yellow flesh.
'Red Duke of York' Early, red-skinned variety with large tubers.
'Picasso' Disease-resistant maincrop variety with white skins.
How to grow Potatoes are referred to as early, second early, and maincrop types according to when they mature. All can be grown in containers and raised beds. Earlier types mature first, so are best for small spaces. Plant "seed" tubers into rich soil, or in 15cm (6in) of compost at the base of a large container. Protect young shoots of early crops from frost. As the stems grow, pile soil at their base to within 10cm (4in) of their tips. Do this 2–3 times to prevent green potatoes.

TURNIPS

- ☀ Full sun or part shade
- ⏳ 6–10 weeks
- 🌡 Late winter to early spring
- 🌱 Early spring to mid-spring
- 🌿 Early spring to late summer
- 🖐 Late spring to early winter
- ↔ 10–15cm (4–6in)
- ★★ Small-space rating

Varieties to try
'Golden Ball' A yellow-skinned variety with a mild flavour.
'Ivory' Very early cropper with sweet-tasting white roots.
'Primera' Best pulled young, it has sweet, purple-tinged white roots.
How to grow For early crops, sow indoors in modules and thin to one per cell, harden them off, and plant out once seedlings are large enough to handle. Alternatively, sow direct every 2–3 weeks from early spring for a constant supply. As turnips prefer cool, moist conditions, keep those sown in summer well watered and shaded – if kept too dry, the roots can become woody. Harvest turnips when they reach golf ball-size. Eat raw or cooked, and use the thinnings in salads.

LEEKS

- ☀ Full sun or part shade
- ⏳ 30–32 weeks
- ⌂ Mid- to late winter
- ▥ Mid-spring to midsummer
- ⚘ Early to mid-spring
- ⚘ Late summer to mid-spring
- ↔ 15–20cm (6–8in)
- ★★ Small-space rating

Varieties to try
'Apollo' A mid-season variety that is resistant to rust.
'King Richard' Grown as an early baby leek, it has long, slim stems.
'Toledo' This late-season leek is bolt-resistant with long stems.
How to grow Leeks do not mind being transplanted, so can be sown in seedbeds, or indoors, to save space while they develop. Sow thinly in small pots or modules in winter, or in a seedbed once the soil is workable, early to mid-spring. Plant out seedlings when pencil-thick and 20cm (8in) tall. Make 15cm (6in) deep planting holes, drop a leek into each one. Do not fill the hole with soil, just water the plants well. As they grow, pile earth around the stems to blanch and support them.

KOHL RABI

- ☀ Full sun or part shade
- ⏳ 9–12 weeks
- ⌂ Early spring
- ▥ Late spring
- ⚘ Mid- to late spring
- ⚘ Summer to autumn
- ↔ 25cm (10in)
- ★★★ Small-space rating

Varieties to try
'Purple Danube' This purple variety has sweet-tasting bulbs.
'Quickstar' A pale green-skinned variety that is bolt-resistant.
'Logo' Ideal for baby bulbs, it is a green-skinned variety.
How to grow For early bulbs, sow indoors into modules in early spring, and plant out about 6 weeks later when the soil is warmer. For a succession of crops, sow directly outdoors every few weeks from mid-spring, thinning to 25cm (10in) apart, and harvest when the size of a tennis ball. For mini kohl rabi, thin to 5cm (2in) apart, and harvest when the size of a golf ball. Kohl rabi is a member of the brassica family – don't sow it where other brassicas have been recently grown.

FLORENCE FENNEL

- ☀ Full sun
- ⏳ 8–24 weeks
- ⌂ Mid-spring
- ▥ Late spring
- ⚘ Late spring
- ⚘ Summer to early autumn
- ↔ 30cm (12in)
- ★ Small-space rating

Varieties to try
'Cantino' This variety has good bolt resistance.
'Zefa Fino' Produces large flattened bulbs with a good flavour.
'Romanesco' A traditional variety with tasty and tender stems.
How to grow Sow seed in large modules or 10cm (4in) pots indoors, 4–6 weeks before the last frosts, then plant them out in a warm and sheltered spot. Alternatively, sow seed directly in the soil during early summer for a later crop. Florence fennel can be tricky to grow, as fluctuations in temperature, or a lack of water, can cause the plants to bolt (flower suddenly), leading to poor bulb development. To prevent bolting, keep your plants moist at all times.

SPRING ONIONS

- ☀ Full sun
- ⏳ 10–14 weeks
- ⌂ Early to mid-spring
- ▥ Late spring to early autumn
- ⚘ Early summer
- ⚘ Midsummer to mid-autumn
- ↔ 1cm (½in)
- ★★ Small-space rating

Varieties to try
'Deep Purple' This variety has a round violet bulbs and green leaves.
'Laser' Slow to form bulbs, this vigorous variety has a mild flavour.
'Lisbon' This traditional variety is good in containers.
How to grow For a constant supply in summer, sow directly outdoors every two weeks from late spring, protecting them from frosts. Thin seedlings to 1cm (½in) apart, keep them watered to avoid the stems becoming bulbous, and harvest when a usable size. Seed can also be sown in late summer for plants to overwinter until spring. Ideal for containers, you can even sow them in pots on a warm, bright windowsill during winter; thin to 4–5 seedlings per 10cm (4in) pot.

GARLIC

- ☀ Full sun
- ⧖ 20–36 weeks
- ⌂ n/a
- 📷 n/a
- 🌱 Mid-autumn to early spring
- 🥄 Late spring to early autumn
- ↔ 20cm (8in)
- ★ Small-space rating

Varieties to try

'Germidour' A mild variety with purple-streaked skins.
'Solent White' Forms large, white, tasty bulbs that store well.
'Sultop' A strongly flavoured variety with pink, easy-to-peel cloves.
How to grow Requiring a cold period to mature, this crop can be grown through winter when beds or containers are empty. Plant cloves directly from mid-autumn to late winter in well drained soil, with their tips showing above the soil surface. Lift them once their leaves yellow in late spring or early summer. Or, plant in early spring to mature from midsummer. You can also plant cloves indoors in pots in early spring if conditions are very wet, for planting out in mid-spring.

CHICORY

- ☀ Full sun or part shade
- ⧖ 10–16 weeks
- ⌂ Early spring and autumn to winter
- 📷 Early summer
- 🌱 Summer
- 🥄 Midsummer to late winter
- ↔ 30cm (12in)
- ★★ Small-space rating

Varieties to try

'Palla Rossa' A bolt-resistant radicchio, with dense red hearts.
'Pan di Zucchero' Sugarloaf type, ideal as a cut-and-come-again.
'Rossa di Treviso Precoce' A radicchio ideal for winter harvesting.
How to grow Red chicory, or radicchio, and green sugarloaf-types are grown in a similar way to lettuce but are hardier. Seed can be started early under cover during spring, ready to plant out in summer, or be sown directly in summer. Plant or thin out the seedlings to about 30cm (12in) apart. Seed can also be sown under cover during autumn and winter, with the plants grown under protection as a cut-and-come-again crop. Water plants well to prevent bolting.

LETTUCES

- ☀ Full sun or part shade
- ⧖ 9–12 weeks
- ⌂ Early spring
- 📷 Mid-spring to late summer
- 🌱 Mid-spring to late summer
- 🥄 Midsummer to autumn
- ↔ 15–35cm (6–14in)
- ★★★ Small-space rating

Varieties to try

'Cocarde' An oak-leaf variety with upright heads.
'Freckles' Cos lettuce with red-speckled green leaves.
'Maravilla de Verano Canasta' Crisp and green, with red tips.
How to grow Sow early crops under cover in spring into modules, thinning each cell to a single plant. Harden off and plant out once large enough to handle. From mid-spring onwards, sow seed directly. If the weather is hot, however, wait until evening, as lettuce will not germinate in temperatures above 25°C (77°F). Thin seedlings, using the thinnings in salads. Harvest by picking the outer leaves or cut the whole head near the base, leaving the stump to re-sprout.

SPINACH

- ☀ Part shade
- ⧖ 6–12 weeks
- ⌂ n/a
- 📷 Late spring to early autumn
- 🌱 n/a
- 🥄 Mid-spring to late autumn
- ↔ 15cm (6in)
- ★★ Small-space rating

Varieties to try

'Barbados' This upright variety has smooth rounded leaves.
'Medania' A prolific variety with soft, deep green leaves.
'Monnopa' Bolt-resistant, its thick leaves are sweet-tasting.
How to grow Plants sown indoors tend to bolt, so sow directly outdoors every three weeks for a succession of leaves. Thin the seedlings to 8cm (3in) apart, then remove alternate plants to use as young leaves and let the remainder mature. Leave late-summer and early-autumn sowings to overwinter for early crops next year. Water this fast-growing leaf crop regularly to prevent bolting. Harvest young leaves for salads from six weeks and mature spinach after ten weeks.

MUSTARD LEAVES

- ☀ Full sun or part shade
- ⧖ 6–8 weeks
- ⌂ Late spring to early summer
- 🌱 Mid- to late summer
- 🌾 Mid- to late summer
- 🍲 Midsummer to late autumn
- ↔ 15–30cm (6–12in)
- ★★★ Small-space rating

Varieties to try
'Golden Streaks' The frilly, lime-green leaves have a sweet flavour.
'Green-in-the-snow' Its jagged leaves have a peppery taste.
'Red Giant' This variety has broad, purple-tinted green leaves.
How to grow Mustard greens are full of vitamins, taste spicier as they mature, and are great in salads and stir-fries. To prevent plants bolting in cool conditions early in the season, sow seed under cover in modules, and plant out when the seedlings are large enough to handle. From midsummer, you can sow directly, using any thinnings as a baby leaf crop. Pick individual leaves or cut the entire head off at the base. Alternatively, sow closely and harvest as a cut-and-come-again crop.

ROCKET

- ☀ Full sun or part shade
- ⧖ 4–12 weeks
- ⌂ Spring and early autumn
- 🌱 Late spring and mid-autumn
- 🌾 Mid-spring to mid-autumn
- 🍲 Early spring to early winter
- ↔ 15cm (6in)
- ★★★ Small-space rating

Varieties to try
'Apollo' Best eaten young, it has large, rounded dark green leaves.
'Pegasus' Mildly peppery, its leaves are large and serrated.
'Sky Rocket' This variety is fast growing and slow to bolt.
How to grow Prone to bolting in hot or dry conditions, and with age, repeat sow for a continuous supply of tender leaves. Sow a new batch once previous seedlings have two true leaves – every 2–3 weeks, depending on the weather. Sow direct outdoors or, in cool areas, sow indoors during spring and autumn into containers, protecting them with fleece. Keep well watered and harvest after two weeks as a cut-and-come-again crop, or after four weeks, picking whole plants.

SWISS CHARD

- ☀ Full sun or part shade
- ⧖ 8–16 weeks
- ⌂ Early to mid-spring
- 🌱 Mid-spring to late summer
- 🌾 Late spring to early summer
- 🍲 Midsummer to spring
- ↔ 20–38cm (8–15in)
- ★★★ Small-space rating

Varieties to try
'Bright Lights' Provides a mixture of brightly coloured stems.
'Charlotte' Resistant to bolting, this variety has bright red stems.
'Fordhook Giant' A large-leaved form with crisp white stems.
How to grow Swiss chard can be cropped for its young tender leaves in summer, or grown over autumn and winter to provide mature stems and leaves for steaming. Sow seed thinly directly into the soil or in modules. Each seed contains a number of seeds, so thin to one plant per sowing position. Sow in spring for a summer harvest, thinning plants to 20cm (8in) apart. For autumn and winter crops, sow in late summer, thinning the plants out to 38cm (15in) apart.

PAK CHOI

- ☀ Full sun
- ⧖ 5–10 weeks
- ⌂ Mid-spring to early summer
- 🌱 Midsummer to late summer
- 🌾 Late spring to early summer
- 🍲 Early summer to mid-autumn
- ↔ 10–25cm (4–10in)
- ★★★ Small-space rating

Varieties to try
'Choko' This variety has slender green leaves.
'Glacier' Bolt-resistant, it has white stems and white-veined leaves.
'Joi Choi' A white-stemmed variety, it resists bolting.
How to grow A useful catch crop, this fast-growing brassica is tasty at all stages, from early thinnings to plump mature heads. Prone to bolting if they become too hot, cold, or dry, sow bolt-resistant varieties indoors in spring at 10–13°C (50–55°F). Sow seed singly and transplant as soon as seedlings can be handled. In summer, sow seed directly outside, thinning to 10cm (4in) apart for baby cut-and-come-again leaves, or 25cm (10in) for mature heads. Water plants regularly.

ENDIVE

- ☀ Full sun or part shade
- ⧖ 12–14 weeks
- ⌂ Mid- to late spring
- 🌱 Early summer to midsummer
- ⚘ Early summer to late summer
- ✋ Midsummer to late autumn
- ↔ 25cm (10in)
- ★★ Small-space rating

Varieties to try
'Frenzy' A frisée-type with compact, self-blanching heads.
'Natacha' Bolt-resistant Batavian variety with broad leaves.
'Pancalieri' A mild, self-blanching, bolt-resistant frisée variety.
How to grow Endive comes in two forms, frisée types with frilly leaves, and the hardier Batavian types with rounded leaves. For a continuous supply, sow a batch every few weeks. Start by sowing indoors in spring to prevent bolting, harden off the seedlings, and plant out once it is warmer. In summer, sow seed directly outside. Once the heads are large enough, cover them with a plate, or tie them shut using string, for ten days to reduce their bitter flavour.

SWEETCORN

- ☀ Full sun
- ⧖ 16–24 weeks
- ⌂ Mid- to late spring
- 🌱 Early summer
- ⚘ Late spring to early summer
- ✋ Late summer to mid-autumn
- ↔ 35–45cm (14–18in) in a block
- ★ Small-space rating

Varieties to try
'Minipop' A baby corn, picked young, and ideal for small spaces.
'Ovation' This is a mid-season variety with large sweet cobs.
'Swift' Dwarf variety, suitable for cool areas. It matures early.
How to grow Sweetcorn is wind-pollinated, so is grown in blocks, and can be underplanted with lower-growing crops, such as lettuces. It needs warmth to germinate and a long growing season. Sow indoors singly in tubes or deep modules in spring to plant out in early summer. In early summer, seed can be sown directly in pairs, then thinned to leave the strongest plants. Support the tall stems by earthing up or with canes. Water well when plants are flowering and the cobs form.

KALE

- ☀ Full sun or part shade
- ⧖ 14–32 weeks
- ⌂ Mid- to late spring
- 🌱 Early summer
- ⚘ Late spring to midsummer
- ✋ Autumn to the following spring
- ↔ 60cm (24in)
- ★★ Small-space rating

Varieties to try
'Cavolo Nero' This variety has slender, dark green, crinkly leaves.
'Redbor' An attractive variety with frilly leaves and purple stems.
'Red Russian' Grown for its serrated grey leaves and purple stems.
How to grow Kale grown for winter cropping can take up a lot of space, so sow in individual pots in mid- to late spring, and plant out in their final positions in midsummer, as space becomes available. Keep plants well watered and provide support as they grow. Kale can be harvested autumn and winter by picking the outer leaves, leaving the inner ones to grow. They can also be harvested as baby leaves during summer and treated as a cut-and-come-again crop.

SPROUTING BROCCOLI

- ☀ Full sun
- ⧖ 34–38 weeks
- ⌂ Late spring
- 🌱 Early summer
- ⚘ Midsummer
- ✋ Late winter to late spring
- ↔ 60cm (24in)
- ★ Small-space rating

Varieties to try
'Red Arrow' This variety is an early cropper, ready to pick in winter.
'Claret' Cropping in spring, this variety matures later.
'Cardinal' Forms upright plants, ready to harvest in spring.
How to grow These are large plants that fill the hungry gap from winter to spring. Sow in individual pots or modules, 1cm (½ in) deep, in late spring, and plant out firmly when space becomes available in midsummer. Seed can also be sown directly outside in early summer, ready to transplant into their final positions. Net young plants to deter pigeons, keep them well watered, and provide support as they grow. In summer, underplant with lettuces and other low-growing crops.

ALPINE STRAWBERRIES

- ☀ Full sun or part shade
- ⌛ Every summer once established
- ⌂ Spring or autumn
- 🌱 Late spring
- ⚘ Mid-spring or early autumn
- ❦ Summer
- ↔ 30–40cm (12–15in)
- ★★ Small-space rating

Varieties to try
'Alexandra' This compact variety is quick to fruit from seed.
'Baron Solemacher' Ideal for containers, it bears dark red fruits.
'Regina' This variety bears masses of large, sweet, scarlet berries.
How to grow These perennials self-seed readily, make good ground cover, and yield a few dainty fruits at a time. Sow seed under cover in spring, grow the seedlings on in pots, then plant them out once the risk of frost has passed. You can also sow directly in rows, but protect seedlings from slugs. Avoid wetting the fruits, which causes them to rot. Remove runners for the best fruits, but propagate fresh plants from runners every 3–4 years. The tiny white flowers are also edible.

STRAWBERRIES

- ☀ Full sun
- ⌛ Every summer once established
- ⌂ n/a
- 🌱 n/a
- ⚘ Spring or autumn
- ❦ Early summer to early autumn
- ↔ 30–40cm (12–16in)
- ★★ Small-space rating

Varieties to try
'Cambridge Favourite' Summer-fruiting with mid-sized berries.
'Flamenco' Perpetual type that bears a large crop of sweet fruits.
'Symphony' A late-season variety, it produces abundant berries.
How to grow These perennials are usually grown from bare-root or pot-grown plants. There are two types: summer-bearers, which produce a single flush of fruits in early to midsummer, and perpetual types that fruit mainly in summer, then sporadically into autumn. Plant outdoors into rich soil or in containers, spacing container plants 15cm (6in) apart. Water well and feed with tomato fertilizer, and keep the fruits off the soil surface using plastic sheeting or dry straw.

AUTUMN RASPBERRIES

- ☀ Full sun or part shade
- ⌛ Every autumn once established
- ⌂ n/a
- 🌱 n/a
- ⚘ Late autumn to early spring
- ❦ Late summer to mid-autumn
- ↔ 35–45cm (14–18in)
- ★★★ Small-space rating

Varieties to try
'All Gold' Bears fragrant, amber berries on self-supporting canes.
'Autumn Bliss' This variety gives good crops of large red berries.
'Polka' Early and free fruiting, its canes are almost thornless.
How to grow Available as bare-root or container-grown plants, they can be grown directly in the soil or in large containers. Autumn raspberries generally don't need support, as they're shorter than summer varieties, and crop on the current season's growth. In spring, mulch to retain soil moisture, then water and feed well for the best fruits. Net plants to protect the berries from birds, and harvest the fruit until the first frosts. Cut down the canes to ground level in late winter.

JAPANESE WINEBERRIES

- ☀ Sun or part shade
- ⌛ Every summer once established
- ⌂ n/a
- 🌱 n/a
- ⚘ Autumn to early spring
- ❦ Mid- to late summer
- ↔ 2.5–3.5m (8–11ft)
- ★★ Small-space rating

Varieties to try
None available – Only the species is grown.
How to grow This is a vigorous shrub that can be planted directly into rich soil, or grown in a large container. Since wineberries fruit on stems produced the previous year, you'll have to wait for at least 18 months for your first berries. When pruned correctly, however, they then fruit every summer. Keep plants well watered, especially when fruiting, and tie in their pink, fuzzy stems to a support, such as trellis or a cane wigwam. To restrict their size in small spaces, train the stems into figures-of-eight, looping them around themselves. Once fruited, cut out the old stems and tie in the new ones to fruit next year.

BLACKBERRIES

- Full sun or part shade
- Every summer once established
- n/a
- n/a
- Autumn to early spring
- Midsummer to early autumn
- 2.5–3.5m (8–11ft)
- ★★ Small-space rating

Varieties to try

'Loch Ness' Compact and thornless, it bears large sweet fruits.
'Silvan' An early variety with large, long, purple-black fruits.
'Waldo' Thornless and compact, this is ideal for containers.

How to grow Blackberries fruit freely on long, clambering stems, although there are compact, thornless varieties available, suitable for large containers. To provide support, plant them against horizontal wires fixed to a fence or between two posts. As fruit is borne on two-year-old canes, train the canes into a fan shape in the first year, then, after fruiting in the second, cut them to the base, retaining the new stems to fruit the following year. Water and feed as per raspberries.

BLUEBERRIES

- Full sun or part shade
- Every summer once established
- n/a
- n/a
- Autumn to early spring
- Late summer to early autumn
- 1.5m (5ft)
- ★ Small-space rating

Varieties to try

'Duke' This is an early and free-fruiting variety.
'Spartan' With an upright habit, it bears richly flavoured fruits.
'Top Hat' A dwarf variety with small and sweet, bright blue berries.

How to grow Ideal for containers, blueberries produce masses of berries, as well as having attractive spring flowers, and bright autumn tints. They must be grown in free-draining acid soil, and should be kept moist at all times using rainwater (tap water is often alkaline). For the best crop, grow two plants, so they can pollinate each other. Mulch in spring and net against birds. After two years, prune each spring, removing congested growth, plus one or two older stems.

APPLES

- Full sun
- Every summer once established
- n/a
- n/a
- Autumn to early spring
- Midsummer to mid-autumn
- 1.8–3.6m (6–12ft)
- ★ Small-space rating

Varieties to try

'Cox's Orange Pippin' A self-fertile apple for eating or cooking.
'Newton Wonder' Bears crisp, tart red fruit for eating and cooking.
'Scrumptious' An early eating variety with sweet red apples.

How to grow For small spaces and containers, choose apples grafted onto dwarfing rootstock M26, and consider training them into space-saving shapes, such as a fan, cordon, or espalier. To ensure the flowers are pollinated and set fruit, grow two trees, unless there is another nearby. Stake freestanding trees, and water well until they are established. Remove fruits in the first year, thereafter thin them to get fewer, but bigger, apples. Depending on form, prune summer or winter.

PEARS

- Full sun
- Every summer once established
- n/a
- n/a
- Autumn to early spring
- Late summer to mid-autumn
- 1.8–3.6m (6–12ft)
- ★ Small-space rating

Varieties to try

'Concorde' Compact and self-fertile, with long dessert pears.
'Doyenné du Comice' Bears sweet, juicy large fruits.
'Onward' A dessert pear with rich, sweet buttery flesh.

How to grow Like apples, choose trees on dwarfing rootstocks and prune them into space-saving forms. You can also choose varieties specially grown for use in containers. Pears require a warm spot and protection from frost to fruit well; they also need one or two pollinating partners, so seek advice on suitable varieties. Stake freestanding trees or train in to their supports. Mulch in spring, thin the fruit, and water well in summer. Depending on the form, prune in summer or winter.

FRENCH SORREL

- ☀ Part shade
- ⧖ 8–18 weeks
- ⌂ Early to mid-spring
- 🌱 Late spring
- 🌿 Mid- to late spring
- 🥄 Summer to autumn
- ↔ 30cm (12in)
- ★★★ Small-space rating

Varieties to try
'De Belleville' This has pale green leaves with a lemony flavour.
'Silver Shield' Forms low mat of silvery green, spear-shaped leaves.
How to grow This hardy perennial adds a lemon or apple tartness to salads, as well as egg, cheese, and fish dishes. Sow batches thinly into modules indoors, or direct outdoors, and thin when the seedlings are large enough to handle. Mulch and water well to keep the soil moist and cool to stop the leaves becoming bitter. Pick young, tender leaves before flowering. Remove the flowers to stop the plants seeding and becoming invasive. Cover with fleece in winter and continue to pick the leaves. Established plants can be divided in spring or autumn.

LOVAGE

- ☀ Full sun or part shade
- ⧖ 42–60 weeks
- ⌂ Late winter to late spring
- 🌱 Mid-spring to early summer
- 🌿 Spring to summer, or in autumn
- 🥄 Late spring to early winter
- ↔ 60cm (24in)
- ★★★ Small-space rating

Varieties to try
None available – Only the species is grown.
How to grow This hardy perennial reaches 2m (6ft) tall, providing celery-flavoured leaves that may be used like spinach in salads, stews, and soups. New plants need time to establish before being picked. Either plant container-grown plants in autumn to pick the following year or, if sowing from seed, only harvest from them in their second season. Sow indoors in modules or direct in rows outside. Pick young, tender leaves early in the season before the flowers appear. Keep the plants moist and cut back in autumn. You can divide mature plants in spring. Note: Eating large amounts may cause stomach upset.

PARSLEY

- ☀ Full sun or part shade
- ⧖ 8–12 weeks
- ⌂ Early spring and early autumn
- 🌱 Late spring to early summer
- 🌿 Late spring to late summer
- 🥄 Year-round
- ↔ 15cm (6in)
- ★★ Small-space rating

Varieties to try
'Laura' A flat-leaved variety with a more intense flavour.
'Lisette' Curly-leaved parsley with bright green, sweet foliage.
'Titan' Flat-leaved variety with lacy, dark green leaves.
How to grow Usually grown as an annual, if sown in regular batches, it can be harvested all year. Sow indoors in spring into modules to avoid root disturbance, keep at a steady 18°C (64°F), and plant out once the risk of frost has passed. In summer, sow directly into moist soil. Keep plants moist, feed weekly with a high-nitrogen fertilizer, and remove any flowers that appear. Late-sown seedlings can be potted up and grown indoors on a bright windowsill.

SWEET CICELY

- ☀ Part shade
- ⧖ 16–20 weeks
- ⌂ n/a
- 🌱 Mid-autumn to late winter
- 🌿 Late winter to autumn
- 🥄 Spring and summer
- ↔ 50–60cm (20–24in)
- ★★★ Small-space rating

Varieties to try
None available – Only the species is grown.
How to grow The ferny leaves of this herb have a sweet aniseed scent, which is great in salads or fruit desserts. It is a large, very hardy perennial, and its seeds need cold to germinate. Sow singly in pots or modules and leave them outside over winter to germinate in spring, or sow seed directly, thinning to leave the strongest plants. Harvest leaves regularly and remove the flat, white flowerheads in summer for new flushes of foliage. You could allow it to flower – stop picking leaves while it does – and use the unripe seeds to add a sharp aniseed tang to salads. Don't allow the seeds to fall, as it self-seeds very readily.

FENNEL

- ☀ Full sun
- ⧖ 16–20 weeks
- ⌂ Early- to mid-spring
- ⬓ Late spring to early summer
- ⚊ Late spring
- ◉ Early summer to mid-autumn
- ↔ 45cm (18in)
- ★★★ Small-space rating

Varieties to try
Foeniculum vulgare Has green foliage and flat, yellow flowerheads.
'Purpureum' This variety has bronze foliage, ageing to grey-green.
How to grow This elegant herb has aniseed-flavoured feathery fronds, stems, and seeds. It can be grown as an annual for its leaves, sowing the seeds directly in spring, or as a perennial for its young leaves and flavoursome seeds. To grow it as a perennial, sow indoors in spring into modules to avoid disturbing the long tap root, then plant out once the risk of frost has passed. Pick leaves regularly before plants flower, or to prolong the harvest, remove the flowering stems. Harvest seed in late summer. Mature plants can be lifted and divided.

BORAGE

- ☀ Full sun
- ⧖ 10–14 weeks
- ⌂ Early spring
- ⬓ Mid- to late spring
- ⚊ Mid- to late spring
- ◉ Early summer to early autumn
- ↔ 20cm (8in)
- ★★★ Small-space rating

Varieties to try
Borago officinalis Blue-flowered with large, fuzzy, grey-green leaves.
'Alba' This variety has white flowers and large green, fuzzy leaves.
How to grow Borage is grown for its edible flowers, which can be added to summer drinks, ice cubes, salads, and desserts. The leaves can also be picked when young and used in salads. Sow seed indoors in pots or modules in spring, harden off, and plant out when large enough to handle, so as not to disturb their tap roots. Seed can also be sown directly and thinned. It is best grown in poor soil or compost to stop it getting leggy. Pick the flowers regularly to keep new buds forming into autumn. Don't allow it to set seed, as it spreads rapidly.

SAGE

- ☀ Full sun
- ⧖ All year once established
- ⌂ n/a
- ⬓ n/a
- ⚊ Autumn and spring
- ◉ Year-round
- ↔ 40cm (16in)
- ★★ Small-space rating

Varieties to try
'Albiflora' This has spikes of white flowers and grey-green leaves.
'Icterina' An attractive shrub with gold variegated foliage.
'Purpurascens' Semi-evergreen with purple-green leaves.
How to grow This shrubby perennial is a classic herb, and one plant will provide a year-round supply of aromatic leaves, to use fresh or dried. It is best bought as a container-grown plant, and requires light, free-draining soil or compost. Pick the leaves regularly, which taste milder before flowering and stronger afterwards. Prune plants after flowering into a neat shape and for new growth. After 3–4 years, sage is best replaced. Buy a new plant or take cuttings in summer.

LAVENDER

- ☀ Full sun
- ⧖ Every summer once established
- ⌂ n/a
- ⬓ n/a
- ⚊ Autumn or spring
- ◉ Early summer to mid-autumn
- ↔ 40–50cm (16–20in)
- ★★ Small-space rating

Varieties to try
'Hidcote' This has dark violet flowers and silvery grey foliage.
'Loddon Pink' Compact with short, greyish-pink flower spikes.
'Munstead' A dwarf plant, with grey leaves and deep blue flowers.
How to grow The highly aromatic leaves and flowers may be used sparingly to flavour sugar, desserts, biscuits, cakes, teas, and oils. Best bought in spring as plugs or container-grown plants, lavender requires free-draining soil or compost. Harvest the flowers during summer and the leaves into autumn. After flowering, shear off all flowered stems, but do not cut into old wood, as it does not resprout. Lavender plants can be short-lived and may need replacing after 4–5 years.

ROSEMARY

- ☀ Full sun
- ⧗ All year once established
- ⌂ n/a
- ▦ n/a
- ⫟ Late spring
- ♣ Year-round
- ↔ 40cm (16in)
- ★★ Small-space rating

Varieties to try
'Green Ginger' Compact and upright with ginger-scented leaves.
'Miss Jessopp's Upright' Has silvery foliage and blue spring flowers.
'Roseus' A pink-flowered variety with bright green foliage.
How to grow An evergreen shrub, rosemary provides a year-round supply of leaves once mature; spring and early summer leaves are more tender. Young plants and some varieties are not fully hardy, so it is best to wait until all risk of frost has passed before planting it outdoors into well drained soil or compost. In cold and exposed areas, plant it in containers that can be brought under cover for winter. Cut back after flowering in spring or summer to keep it neat and prompt new growth.

SWEET BASIL

- ☀ Full sun
- ⧗ 6–8 weeks
- ⌂ Early spring to early summer
- ▦ Early to midsummer
- ⫟ Early to midsummer
- ♣ Early summer to autumn
- ↔ 25cm (10in)
- ★★★ Small-space rating

Varieties to try
'Cinnamon' This has purple-brown foliage with a spicy taste.
'Sweet Green' Ideal for pesto, it has mint- and clove-scented leaves.
'Purple Ruffles' It has strongly flavoured frilly, purple-black foliage.
How to grow This tender annual needs hot, dry conditions; it often grows best on a sunny windowsill or under glass. Sow in batches indoors at a minimum of 18°C (64°F), cover thinly, and water seedlings sparingly to avoid rot. Sow in midsummer for plants to last into winter. Sow direct only in warm, sheltered soil or containers. Pick basil tips regularly to keep it compact and producing new leaves. Water plants cautiously, and never in the evening, as basil hates having wet feet.

AFRICAN BASIL

- ☀ Full sun
- ⧗ 12–28 weeks
- ⌂ n/a
- ▦ n/a
- ⫟ Early summer
- ♣ Early to late summer
- ↔ 30–40cm (12–16in)
- ★★ Small-space rating

Varieties to try
None available – Only the species is grown.
How to grow This herb has deliciously tasty leaves, similar to sweet basil, and its purple spires of flowers are much loved by bees. Unlike traditional basil, it is a tender perennial, and is only available as plugs or container-grown plants, as it does not produce seed. It needs well drained soil or compost, and is ideal for containers, although should not be planted out until the risk of frost has passed. Plants can be cut back and brought under cover for winter. To grow new plants, take 10–15cm (4–6in) cuttings during spring. Insert them into gritty compost, and water sparingly. They will root in a matter of weeks.

MINT

- ☀ Full sun or part shade
- ⧗ Every summer once established
- ⌂ n/a
- ▦ n/a
- ⫟ Mid-spring to early summer
- ♣ Early to late summer
- ↔ 30–40cm (12–16in)
- ★★★ Small-space rating

Varieties to try
Ginger mint (*Mentha* x *gracilis*) It has spicy variegated leaves.
Spearmint (*M. spicata*) Fresh-tasting leaves with purple flowers.
Apple mint (*M. suaveolens*) Hairy green foliage with a zingy taste.
How to grow This is a very useful herb, and one plant of any variety is all you need, as they are rampant growers. It is best bought in spring as a plug or a container-grown plant. All types spread quickly, so they are best grown in large containers, which can be plunged into borders to control their spreading roots. Keep plants well watered, pick young leaves regularly, and cut back tired stems in summer to encourage new growth. There is a wide range of species and varieties available.

FRENCH TARRAGON

- ☀ Full sun
- ⊠ Every summer once established
- ⌂ n/a
- ⬒ n/a
- 🌱 Spring
- 🍂 Summer to early autumn
- ↔ 60cm (24in)
- ★★★ Small-space rating

Varieties to try
None available – Only the species is grown.
How to grow This herb has narrow, silver-green leaves that have a distinctive mint-anise flavour. Difficult to grow from seed in cool climates, it is best bought as a container-grown plant. It is suitable for growing in borders or containers, and needs full sun and well drained, alkaline or neutral soil or compost. Tarragon hates cold, wet conditions, and is not fully hardy, so should be protected from excessive winter wet and hard frosts. Plants grown in containers could be brought under cover. Although they look similar, do not confuse this with the more vigorous but less flavoursome Russian tarragon.

CHIVES

- ☀ Full sun
- ⊠ Every summer once established
- ⌂ Late winter to late spring
- ⬒ Late spring
- 🌱 Early spring to midsummer
- 🍂 Late spring to mid-autumn
- ↔ 15cm (6in)
- ★★★ Small-space rating

Varieties to try
'Black Isle Blush', This variety has mauve flowers with pink centres.
'Silver Chimes' Dwarf variety with white flowers. Strongly flavoured.
'Forescate' Grown for its pink flowers and tasty blue-green leaves.
How to grow A hardy perennial, chives are a natural cut-and-come-again crop. Sow indoors thinly in trays, prick out in threes or fours into pots to grow on, then plant out once frosts have passed. Plants can also be kept under cover for early crops. Seed can also be sown directly outside in summer. Begin harvesting once the leaves reach 15cm (6in) tall, and cut them back every two months to promote tender new growth. The attractive flowers are also good to eat.

DILL

- ☀ Full sun
- ⊠ 8–10 weeks
- ⌂ Late winter to early spring
- ⬒ Late spring
- 🌱 Mid-spring to midsummer
- 🍂 Summer
- ↔ 20cm (8in)
- ★★★ Small-space rating

Varieties to try
'Bouquet' A dwarf form with highly aromatic, ferny foliage.
'Compatto' Dwarf variety, suitable for containers.
'Dukat' This form has sweetly flavoured, blue-green leaves.
How to grow This frost-hardy annual has a long tap root, so grows best if sown directly. Sow seed outdoors in batches for a constant supply. Barely cover the seed, and protect early seedlings under cloches until all risk of frost has passed. For an early crop, sow indoors in modules and thin each to the strongest seedling. Harvest leaves once plants reach 30cm (12in) tall, cutting the whole plant. You can also use the edible flowers and seeds. Keep the plants well watered.

POT MARJORAM

- ☀ Full sun
- ⊠ Every summer once established
- ⌂ n/a
- ⬒ n/a
- 🌱 Late spring to midsummer
- 🍂 Midsummer to mid-autumn
- ↔ 25cm (10in)
- ★★★ Small-space rating

Varieties to try
'Acorn Bank' A yellow-leaved form with pink flowers.
'Compactum' Forms a low mound of dark green, aromatic leaves.
'Country Cream' Has variegated green and cream foliage.
How to grow A hardy perennial, oregano is an essential herb in Mediterranean cooking. Tricky and slow to raise from seed, it is best bought as plugs or container-grown plants. It is ideal for containers and windowboxes, or to plant alongside a path, and needs full sun and well drained soil. Harvest the leaves before the flower buds open, when they taste at their best. This herb is often confused with sweet marjoram, which is less hardy, but still worth growing.

THYME

- ☀ Full sun
- ⧖ Every summer once established
- ⌂ n/a
- ▥ n/a
- ↯ Late spring to early summer
- ☙ Late spring to early winter
- ↔ 30cm (12in)
- ★★★ Small-space rating

Varieties to try
'Golden King' Lemon-scented with golden-edged foliage.
'Orange Balsam' Has orange- and thyme-scented leaves.
'Silver Queen' A cream-variegated variety with mauve flowers.
How to grow Evergreen thyme has a creeping habit, and is ideal for planting in very small but sunny places. It is slow to grow from seed, so is best bought as container-grown plants. There are many varieties to choose – some with distinctive flavours. Pick only a few leaves until the plant is established. The flavour is best before flowering; trim plants hard after flowering to prompt fresh growth. Plants require well drained soil and can be short-lived.

CORIANDER

- ☀ Full sun or part shade
- ⧖ 4–8 weeks for the leaves
- ⌂ Early spring and autumn
- ▥ Mid-spring
- ↯ Mid-spring to midsummer
- ☙ Late spring to early winter
- ↔ 25–30cm (10–12in)
- ★★★ Small-space rating

Varieties to try
'Calypso' Fast-growing, the leaves can be cut down 3 or 4 times.
'Confetti' This variety has delicate, feathery, sweet-tasting foliage.
'Leisure' Good for containers, it has large, tasty leaves and flowers.
How to grow This annual can be grown in part-shade for the most flavoursome leaves, or in full sun for its spicy seeds. Early crops can be sown under cover in spring, although may bolt when planted out, so seeds are best sown directly outside in monthly batches. Seed can also be sown in pots during autumn to grow through winter indoors on a bright windowsill. Cut leaf crops regularly and keep them moist to prevent bolting. Support top-heavy seed crops with canes.

OXALIS TRIANGULARIS

- ☀ Full sun or part shade
- ⧖ 8–10 weeks
- ⌂ n/a
- ▥ n/a
- ↯ Early summer
- ☙ Midsummer to autumn
- ↔ 30cm (12in)
- ★ Small-space rating

Varieties to try
None available – only the species is grown
How to grow Often used as a house plant, this tender perennial can be planted outside for summer, and grown for its lemon-flavoured, purple leaves and its attractive pale pink flowers. Buy container-grown plants in late spring, and plant them into free-draining soil or compost in beds or containers after the last frost. Keep plants well watered and deadhead them frequently to encourage more flowers to grow. Pick the leaves and flowers sparingly, when required, and add them to salads. Plants can be lifted in autumn and brought indoors until spring, when larger plants can be divided.

NASTURTIUMS

- ☀ Full sun
- ⧖ 10–12 weeks
- ⌂ Mid-spring
- ▥ Late spring to early summer
- ↯ Late spring and early summer
- ☙ Summer to autumn
- ↔ 45cm (18in)
- ★★★ Small-space rating

Varieties to try
'Indian Chief' Climber with bright red flowers and dark green leaves.
'Alaska' A variegated form with attractive white-splashed foliage.
'Black Velvet' Bears sumptuous deep red flowers.
How to grow This annual is grown from seed, sown under cover in pots in spring, or directly outside once the risk of frost has passed. It has a trailing or climbing habit, and can be trained up a support or left to creep amongst your plants. It grows well in most soils, even poor soil, and is suitable for borders and containers. The flowers, leaves, and fresh seeds are all edible, and have a strong peppery taste, especially the seeds. Nasturtiums will self-seed readily.

CALIFORNIAN POPPIES

- Full sun
- 10 weeks
- n/a
- Mid-spring to early summer
- n/a
- Summer
- 15–20cm (6–8in)
- ★★★ Small-space rating

Varieties to try

'Chrome Queen' Pale yellow flowers with feathery foliage.
'Red Chief' Vibrant red-flowered variety with blue-green leaves.
'Orange King' Has rich orange flowers and feathery leaves.

How to grow The seeds of this annual are sown directly where they are to flower, either in well drained borders or in containers, during mid-spring. Sow in a couple of batches a few weeks apart to extend the flowering season, thinning the seedlings to 15–20cm (6–8in) apart. Pick the flowers as required, adding the petals to salads and summer drinks. Deadhead the plants frequently to encourage repeat flowering. Californian poppies will readily self-seed, returning year after year.

POT MARIGOLDS

- Full sun
- 10–12 weeks
- Early spring
- Mid-spring
- Mid- to late spring
- Summer to autumn
- 30cm (12in)
- ★★★ Small-space rating

Varieties to try

'Neon' This variety has deep orange petals, tipped with red.
'Orange Porcupine' The orange flowers have quilled petals.
'Orange Prince' Free-flowering with open, deep orange flowers.

How to grow This annual is easy to grow from seed, and there are many varieties to try. In early spring, sow seed into small pots or modules under cover, and thin the seedlings to leave the strongest. Harden them off and plant out 30cm (12in) apart. Seed can also be sown directly where they are to flower, in borders or containers. Keep plants well watered and deadhead frequently. Pot marigolds are great for companion planting, and as garnishes in salads and other dishes.

VIOLAS

- Full sun or part shade
- 8–24 weeks
- Spring or autumn
- Late spring
- Spring
- Summer to early autumn
- 45cm (18in)
- ★★★ Small-space rating

Varieties to try

'Heart's ease' (*V. tricolor*) has dainty purple, yellow, and white flowers.
'Pat Kavanagh' This variety has yellow flowers with mauve edges.
'Maggie Mott' Has silvery mauve blooms with cream centres.

How to grow Violas are usually bought as plants, as they are so readily available and cheap to buy. Plant in the garden or in pots in mid- to late spring and, if regularly deadheaded, they should flower throughout summer. Perennial varieties will often flower into autumn, and many have a wonderfully sweet scent. Pick the flowers as you need them and add them to salads and summer drinks. Many varieties will self-seed freely, so you may only need to buy them once.

SWEET WILLIAMS

- Full sun
- 32 weeks from plants
- n/a
- Early to midsummer
- Autumn
- Late spring to early summer
- 25cm (10in)
- ★★ Small-space rating

Varieties to try

'Auricula Eyed' Produces clusters of fringed pink and white flowers.
'Sweet Red' Dwarf form with red flowers that is ideal for containers.
'Dianbunda Red Picotee' This variety may bloom in its first year.

How to grow Sweet William is a biennial that is normally bought as year-old plants in autumn to flower the following spring. It can also be grown from seeds, which will flower in their second year, although you will need spare space for them to grow on in the meantime. Its flowers have a delicious clove-like scent, and can be used to add colour to salads and drinks. Keep the plants well watered and deadhead them regularly. Discard spent plants after flowering.

Common pests

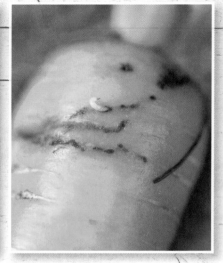

Snails and slugs Coming out mostly at night and during wet spells, these pests will attack your crops at every stage of growth, weakening or even killing them. Apply pellets or use slug and snail barriers and traps.

Cabbage white caterpillars Despite their name, these caterpillars feed on most members of the brassica family, stripping their leaves to skeletons. Net your plants to prevent the adults laying eggs on your crops.

Carrot fly larvae These tiny maggots burrow into the roots of carrots and turnips, creating mush-filled tunnels. Net plants to prevent the adults laying eggs near your plants or grow resistant varieties.

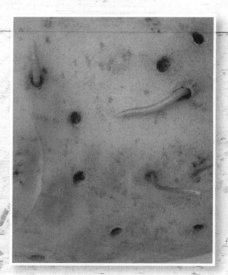

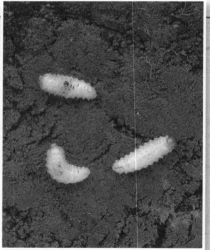

Wireworms Larvae of the click beetle, these soil-dwelling grubs feed on the roots of seedlings, killing them, and burrow into potatoes and onions. There is no treatment. Simply remove the pests if you find them.

Vine weevil grubs These small cream-coloured maggots feed on the roots of many crops, especially those grown in containers. Treat containers with a nematode solution and remove any grubs you find in your pots.

Birds Newly planted brassica plants are often stripped of their leaves by pigeons (*above*). Ripening fruit will also be targeted by many types of bird. Net your plants to soil level to ensure birds cannot sneak below.

Aphids Also known as black- or greenfly, these sap-sucking insects form large colonies, and can weaken or kill your plants. Treat with a suitable insecticide, or wash them off and encourage natural predators.

Cats, dogs, and foxes Whether you like them or not, these can cause significant harm to your crops by digging them up or urinating on them. Use deterrents to keep them away, or protect plants with nets and barriers.

Flea beetle These tiny black beetles, which jump from your plants when disturbed, feed on leaves, especially of seedlings, peppering them with holes. Cover plants with fine fleece as a barrier or use a suitable insecticide.

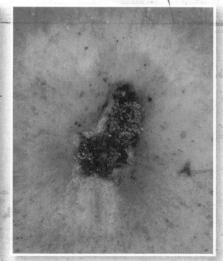

Pea and bean weevils Creating small notches in the leaves of pea and bean plants, the damage often looks worse than it is. If your plants are weakened, however, treat them using a suitable insecticide.

Cabbage root fly larvae These small maggots feed on the roots of newly planted members of the brassica family, causing them to wilt and die. Protect seedlings by fitting barrier collars when planting (*above*).

Codling moth caterpillars Attacking apples and pears, these pests burrow into the fruits, creating tunnels, and spoiling them. Lure the egg-laying adults away from your trees using codling moth traps in late spring.

Common diseases and disorders

Blight This fungal disease attacks potatoes, causing brown patches on the leaves, which suddenly wilt, and the tubers may rot. It also affects tomatoes, causing the fruits to turn brown. Infected plants are best discarded.

Blossom end rot A disorder rather than a disease, the ends of tomato and courgette fruits decay, which spreads to the whole fruit. It is caused by erratic watering. Simply water your plants more regularly.

Damping off This fungal disease kills seedlings, most commonly raised indoors, by causing their stems to collapse. To prevent this, sow into new compost, water with tap water, and keep seedlings well ventilated.

Splitting tomato skins This problem results from erratic watering while the fruits are developing. The split fruits may then also rot. Prevent splitting by keeping your plants evenly moist at all times while in fruit.

Clubroot Affecting members of the brassica family, this soil-borne disease distorts their roots, causing the plants to wilt and grow weakly – if not die. Grow resistant varieties and rotate your crops annually.

Grey mould This disease affects a wide variety of crops, including fruit. It forms downy grey patches of mould on the leaves, stems, flowers, or fruits, which then decay. Remove affected growth to prevent spread.

Downy mildew Most common in wet weather, the leaves of many crops develop brown patches on the top, with pale mould beneath. Remove infected growth, avoid wetting the leaves, and improve airflow.

Powdery mildew Most common in dry spells when plants are stressed, powdery white patches appear on leaves and stems, weakening the plant. Remove affected growth and keep plants well watered.

Rust Infected plants develop orange-brown pustules on the leaves, become weak, and may die. Avoid using nitrogen-rich fertilizers, remove affected growth, and keep beds free of plant debris. Fungicides can be applied.

Brown rot on fruit This mostly affects damaged fruits, which soften, turn brown, and shrivel up. White pustules may then appear. Protect fruits from bird damage, remove affected fruits, and apply fungicide.

Bolting This refers to plants, often leaf crops, suddenly flowering, after which they soon die, spoiling the harvest. It is caused by heat or moisture stress. Sow seeds at the recommended time and keep plants moist.

Scorch The leaves of any plant can be damaged by strong wind (*above*) or by hot sunlight, causing dead, brown patches. Choose the best place grow your crops, keep them moist, and provide shelter if required.

Common garden weeds

Ragwort This annual weed forms a large rosette of crinkle-edged dark green leaves, and produces tall stems of yellow flowers in summer. It seeds very freely, so should be removed before it flowers.

Annual meadow-grass This annual grass grows and flowers quickly, and soon colonizes bare soil. It is easily controlled by hoeing around your plants regularly. Do not allow it to flower and set seeds.

Bindweed This is a rampant, climbing perennial weed that spreads via creeping roots. It will quickly smother crops if not controlled. Do not dig it up, as this will spread the roots – use a systemic weedkiller instead.

Creeping thistle A tough perennial weed, problem plants are most likely on existing vegetable patches. Kill them at root level with a systemic weedkiller. Seedlings can appear on new beds and can be easily hoed off.

Hairy bittercress This annual spreads very rapidly by firing its seeds far and wide from exploding pods. Seedlings flower within a matter of weeks. Hoe them off before they have time to flower, and pull them from pots.

Dandelions A perennial weed, mature plants are most likely on established plots, where the long tap roots need to be pulled from the ground whole. It self-seeds freely, so seedlings can occur anywhere. Hoe them off.

Goosegrass This clinging weed will quickly scrabble among your crops, and can smother smaller plants. Pull it up by hand before it has the chance to flower and produce its sticky seed pods. Hoe seedlings off.

Groundsel A quick-growing annual weed, it will rapidly colonize any bare earth, as well as containers. It flowers and sets seeds in a matter of weeks, and spreads readily. Pull up mature plants by hand and hoe off seedlings.

Shepherd's purse This annual weed produces long spikes of tiny white flowers that lead to characteristic heart-shaped seed pods. Quick to grow and flower, pull it up before it has time to produce seeds.

Creeping buttercup A perennial, this colourful weed spreads via its creeping roots, and can soon weave itself among your crops. Seedlings can be hoed off but treat mature plants with a systemic weedkiller.

Dock Mature plants of this perennial weed are more common on established plots, and have deep roots that are hard to pull up. Treat them with systemic weedkiller. Seedlings can be pulled by hand or hoed off.

Stinging nettle This perennial weed is common in unused urban plots. It forms dense mats of roots that easily re-grow, so treat with a systemic weedkiller. Hoe off seedlings or pull by hand, wearing gloves.

Useful resources
Seeds & plants

Chiltern Seeds
Crowmarsh Battle Barns,
114 Preston Crowmarsh,
Wallingford,
OX10 6SL
01491 824675
www.chilternseeds.co.uk

D.T. Brown
Bury Road,
Newmarket,
Cambridge
CB8 7PQ
0845 371 0532
dtbrownseeds.co.uk

Dobies
Long Road,
Paignton,
Devon
TQ4 7SX
0333 400 7623
www.dobies.co.uk

Edwin Tucker
Brewery Meadow,
Stonepark,
Ashburton,
Devon
TQ13 7DG
01364 652403
www.edwintucker.com

Marshall/Unwins
Alconbury Hill,
Huntingdon,
Cambridge
PE28 4HY
Marshalls 0844 557 6700
Unwins 0844 573 8400
www.marshalls-seeds.co.uk
www.unwins.co.uk

Mr Fothergill's
Gazeley Road,
Kentford,
Suffolk
CB8 7QB
0845 371 0518
www.mr-fothergills.co.uk

Plant World Seeds
St Marychurch Road,
Newton Abbot,
Devon
TQ12 4SE
01803 872939
www.plant-world-seeds.com

Seeds of Italy
A1 Phoenix Industrial Estate,
Rosslyn Cresent,
Harrow,
Middlesex
HA1 2SP
0208 427 5020
www.seedsofitaly.com

Simpson's Seeds
The Walled Garden Nursery,
Horningsham,
Warminster,
Wiltshire
BA12 7NQ
01985 845004
www.simpsonsseeds.co.uk

Suffolk Herbs
Monks Farm,
Coggeshall Road,
Kelvedon,
Essex
CO5 9PG
01376 570 000
www.suffolkherbs.com

Suttons Seeds
Woodview Road,
Paignton,
Devon
TQ4 7NG
0844 922 2899
www.suttons.co.uk

The Organic Gardening Catalogue
Riverdene Business Park,
Molesey Road,
Hersham,
Surrey
KT12 4RG
01932 253666
www.organiccatalogue.com

The Real Seed Catalogue
PO Box 18,
Newport,
Pembrokeshire
SA65 0AA
01239 821107
www.realseeds.co.uk

Thompson & Morgan
Poplar Lane,
Ipswich,
Suffolk
IP8 3BU
0844 573 1818
www.thompson-morgan.com

Victoriana Nursery Gardens
Buck Street
Challock,
Ashford,
Kent
TN25 4DG
01233 740529
www.victoriananursery.co.uk

Plants & sundries

Blackmoor Nurseries
Blackmoor,
Liss,
Hampshire
GU33 6BS
01420 477978
www.blackmoor.co.uk

Chris Bowers & Sons
Whispering Trees Nurseries,
Wimbotsham,
Norfolk
PE34 3QB
01366 388752
www.chrisbowers.co.uk

Crocus
Nursery Court,
London Road,
Windlesham,
Surrey
GU20 6LQ
01387 720880
www.crocus.co.uk

Deacon's Nursery
Moor View,
Godshill,
Isle of Wight
PO38 3HW
01983 840750
www.deaconsnurseryfruits.co.uk

Herbal Haven
Coldhams Farm,
Rickling,
Saffron Walden,
Essex
CB11 3YL
Tel: 01799 540695
www.herbalhaven.com

Ken Muir
Honeypot Farm,
Rectory Road,
Weeley Heath,
Clacton-on-Sea,
Essex
CO16 9BJ
01255 830181
www.kenmuir.co.uk

Vegetable Plants Direct
12 Somerville Road,
Sandford,
Winscombe,
North Somerset
BS25 5RP
07840 106983
www.vegetableplantsdirect.co.uk

Burgon & Ball
La Plata Works,
Holme Lane
Sheffield,
South Yorkshire
S6 4JY
0114 233 8262
www.burgonandball.com

Harrod Horticultural
Pinbush Road,
Lowestoft,
Suffolk
NR33 7NL
0845 402 5300
www.harrodhorticultural.com

Ladybird Plant Care
The Glasshouses,
Fletching Common,
Newick,
Lewes,
East Sussex
BN8 4JJ
www.ladybirdplantcare.co.uk

Two Wests & Elliott
Unit 4 Carrwood Road,
Sheepbridge Industrial Estate,
Chesterfield,
Derbyshire
S41 9RH
01508 548395
www.twowests.co.uk

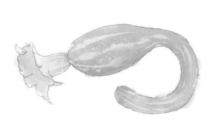

Index

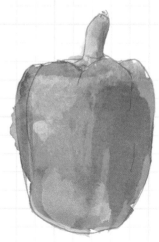

Acknowledgments

Picture credits

The publisher would like to thank the following for their kind permission to reproduce their photographs:

Lucy Claxton (c) Dorling Kindersley 14 FBL; Lucy Claxton (c) Dorling Kindersley 25 CLA; (c) Alan Buckingham 30 FBR; Brian North (c) Dorling Kindersley, Courtesy of RHS Chelsea Flower Show 2009 36 CRB; (c) Alan Buckingham 37 CRA; Peter Anderson (c) Dorling Kindersley, Courtesy of RHS Hampton Court Flower Show 40 CRA; (c) Alan Buckingham 44 FCLB; (c) Jerry Young 55 CRA; Mark Winwood (c) Dorling Kindersley, Courtesy of RHS Wisley 55 FBL; Getty: Reggie Casagrande / Photodisc 57 FCRA; Brian North (c) Dorling Kindersley, Courtesy of RHS Chelsea Flower Show 2011 75 C; Mark Winwood (c) Dorling Kindersley, Courtesy of RHS Wisley 107 FCLA; Joanne Doran (c) Dorling Kindersley, Courtesy of RHS Hampton Court Flower Show 2011 117 C; Peter Anderson (c) Dorling Kindersley, Courtesy of RHS Chelsea Flower Show 2009 157 C; Peter Anderson (c) Dorling Kindersley, Courtesy of RHS Hampton Court Flower Show 183 CRB; Peter Anderson (c) Dorling Kindersley, Courtesy of RHS Hampton Court Flower Show 183 CLB; Peter Anderson (c) Dorling Kindersley, Courtesy of RHS Hampton Court Flower Show 2010 183 CRA; Peter Anderson (c) Dorling Kindersley, Courtesy of RHS Hampton Court Flower Show 201 BL; Joanne Doran (c) Dorling Kindersley, Courtesy of RHS Hampton Court Flower Show 2011 211 CLA; Joanne Doran (c) Dorling Kindersley, Courtesy of RHS Hampton Court Flower Show 2011 221 CRB; Peter Anderson (c) Dorling Kindersley, Courtesy of RHS Hampton Court Flower Show 2010 221 CLA; Lucy Claxton (c) Dorling Kindersley 225 TR; Peter Anderson (c) Dorling Kindersley, Courtesy of RHS Hampton Court Flower Show 2010 229 TR; (c) Alan Buckingham 233 FCLB; (c) Alan Buckingham 233 CRB; (c) Alan Buckingham 234 CRB; (c) Alan Buckingham 244 FCRB; (c) Alan Buckingham 245 FCLB;

Dorling Kindersley would like to thank:

Photography Peter Anderson
Editorial support Esther Ripley and Annalise Evans
Design support Eleanor Bates, Vanessa Hamilton, and Amy Keast
Proofreading Constance Novis
Indexing Vanessa Bird

DK would also like to give special thanks to the following for their kind help in producing this book:

Bruno Lacey and his colleagues at Urban Growth, London, for helping to create and maintain many of the raised beds featured.

Tom Wheatcroft and his colleagues at Capel Manor College, London, for helping to create and maintain many of the projects shown.

Clare Dyson at Pro-Veg Seeds Ltd, Cambridge, for supplying plants.

Faulks and Cox Ltd, Leicestershire, for supplying many of the containers used.